Launch

The Website Design Workbook

CJ Hallock

Notes from CJ

1. This is a workbook so you may want to use a pencil in case if you need to change something.

2. If you take my recommendation for your hosting, domain or any other products (MyHostLink.com, HostYak, etc.) I may receive compensation.

3. If you do better with video tutorials, you can go to WebDesignWebinar.com and register to watch me build a website from the ground up. (I do use a shortcut during this so a lot of the steps used in this book are not used because I've created a template to speed up the process.)

ISBN-13: 978-1719359474
ISBN-10: 1719359474

Welcome to the Website Design Blueprint

Get a complete list of all tools & resources mentioned in this book at DigiToolBag.com

Join me for a FREE complete video walk-through as I build a website with the steps covered in this book. (Disclaimer: I do use a shortcut in the webinar to cut the time needed to build a website in half) Sign up here → WebDesignWebinar.com

In this website design checklist & workbook, you will follow along and check off each of the steps needed to build a professional website with WordPress.

This is a checklist I have put together for myself to use when I'm building out client websites. I've just made it look pretty for you all! I hope you enjoy!

I wanted to cover a little bit before we dig into the workbook. I have been building websites with WordPress since 2009. I sold my first WordPress website in 2010.

The reason for me putting together this book and all the other training & resources is because over the last 10 years in helping small businesses and professionals, I continue to see people get lied to and end up with websites that are neither easy on the eye or converting business.

So I decided that it would be a lot harder to scale one website at a time and that doing this would be a great way for me to help people make their own website.

So … Here We Go!

PS. Throughout this workbook you will find bullet journal pages along with some other "workbook" style pages. Please use these moving forward to help with the process.

PPS. You will find your password log on the opposite page. If you do decide to use it, please be sure that you keep this workbook in a secure location to prevent people from gaining access to your website and online accounts.

Password Log

Account/Website	Username/Email	Password/Pin
Gmail		
YourEmail@You.com		
Your Website Login		
InMotionHosting		
HostYak		
Elementor		
DigiToolBag		
Aweber		

Password Log

Account/Website	Username/Email	Password/Pin

☐ Find a Good Handle/Domain With Knowem.com

Most people rush out as soon as they have a business idea and buy the .com they want and don't think about the side effects that come with not doing any research. This is why I use Knowem.com. You can use their free tool to find the ideal handle/domain.

This will let you know if the name you are wanting is available for purchase as the .com domain along with checking the username availability with different social media platforms & trademark status. This will help you & save you a lot of time & money!

EXAMPLE: If you run ACME Home Improvement, you'd want to check acmehomeimprovement. After a search I see that it is too long for a few of the social platforms and the .com is already registered. So I would continue to try different variations. Finally I found acmehometn.com was available. The USPTO Trademark Database came back with the trademark available! Last thing that would make this name great? It is available on all social media sites. At the time of me writing this "Facebook" is the only platform where it is not available, so I would continue until I find one that is good for everything. (Sorry I don't want to waste our time so I'm stopping here.)

Enter your personal username or business name in the "enter name here" box above and click Search. Please note Social Media usernames and accounts cannot contain spaces, symbols, or anything other than letters and numbers.

Quick Search of the Most Popular Social Networks:

Blogger	Available	**BuzzFeed**	Available	**Dailymotion**	Available
Etsy	Available			foursquare	Available
HubPages	Available	imgur	Available	issuu	Available
Linked		LiveJournal	Available	my	Available
photobucket	Available	Pinterest	Available	reddit	Available
Scribd	Available			tumblr.	Available
twitter	Available	TypePad	Available	vimeo	Available
		You Tube	Available		

Twitter Facebook LinkedIn Google+ Pocket Email

→ **Busy?**

Don't be one of those companies that get stuck with a different username on every Social Network - Make your Social Branding consistent, and let us Secure your Brand on up to 300 Social Networks today!

Next Step: These 25 networks are just the start! KnowEm's Social Brand Search Engine checks over 500 social networks for your brand or username, categorized by niche markets:

▸ CLICK HERE TO SEARCH OVER 500 MORE SOCIAL NETWORKS

Quick Search of the Most Popular Domain Extensions:

acmehometn.com Available	acmehometn.net Available
acmehometn.org Available	acmehometn.info Available
acmehometn.biz Available	acmehometn.tel Available
acmehometn.mobi Available	acmehometn.name Available
acmehometn.co Available	acmehometn.ag Available
acmehometn.tv Available	acmehometn.me Available
acmehometn.travel Available	

Next Step: Did you think we only searched a dozen domain extensions? No way! Our domain search lets you check for the availability of your domain name on *over 150 more domain extenstions on one page*, broken down by geographic region:

▸ SEARCH OVER 150 MORE DOMAIN EXTENSIONS

Search of the USPTO Trademark Database:

 Congratulations, your Trademark is Available!

The name you searched for, **acmehometn**, is **not located** in the USPTO database! This means that no one else has trademarked the term **acmehometn** ... yet!

You can register it now for only $158 + the standard $325 USPTO Filing Fee.

Next Step: KnowEm offers a complete and exhaustive search of the USPTO Trademark Database. If you're looking to register a trademark on your business, product or brand name, KnowEm has it covered:

▸ SEARCH THE COMPLETE TRADEMARK DATABASE

Enter your personal username or business brand name in the "enter name here" box above and click Search. Then click "Check This Category" to further specify the search for your brand name's availability in each section. Please note Social Media usernames and accounts cannot contain spaces, symbols, or anything other than letters and numbers.

Tired of checking and registering all these names yourself?
Want to claim your Brand on all of these sites before someone else does?
Then you want our Social Profile Creation Service! Just give us your personal brand, product or business information, and a highly trained Social Media Specialist assigned to you will begin creating up to 300 Social Media Profiles for you, today!

Since we launched in 2009 the KnowEm team has helped to reserve over 650,000 profiles and reported back to our clients over 50,000 issues of brand squatting and/or misrepresentation of a brand, username or trademarked term. Don't be one of those companies that get stuck with a different handle on every Social Network - Make your Social Branding consistent, and reserve your name today!

Blogging

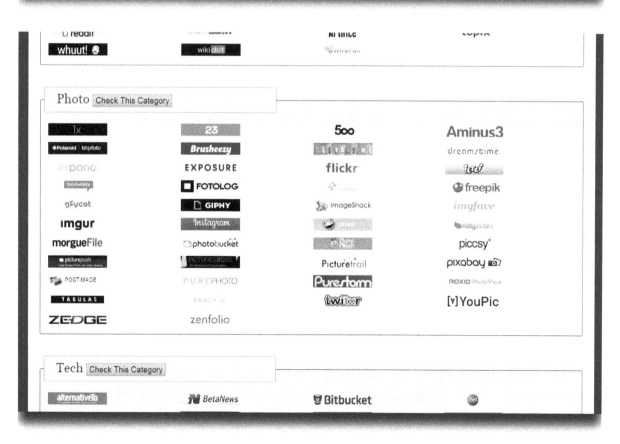

Photo Check This Category

Tech Check This Category

NOTE: While you may want to use a different extensions I highly recommend that you **ONLY MOVE FORWARD WHEN YOU FIND A .COM**. If you want to use a .net .org or one of the fun extensions such as .yeah, you can. But, you would be better getting the .com and building your website there then forward the other domain(s) to your main website. (More on that later)

If you do not see a social media site you want to check on the main page (like Instagram) you can go to the "Social Networks" tab and check each category of social sites. It automatically checks the "Blogging" category for you. If you want to check each of the other categories all you need to do is click "Check This Category" button for the desired category.

Run a search on Knowem.com with your desired username/domain and use the form below to track your progress until you find the perfect name for your business.

Desired Name	Social Availability	Domain Availability	Trademark Availability
	Yes | No	Yes | No	Yes | No
	Yes | No	Yes | No	Yes | No
	Yes | No	Yes | No	Yes | No
	Yes | No	Yes | No	Yes | No
	Yes | No	Yes | No	Yes | No
	Yes | No	Yes | No	Yes | No
	Yes | No	Yes | No	Yes | No

Now that you have a name in mind, the next step is to register the domain and all of that fun stuff. Use this section to notate the Username/Domain you selected.

Username/Domain To Use: _____

***Please don't move forward until you have done this and found a name that you can use on the social media sites you plan to use, register as a .com domain & is not trademarked by anyone.

Before you move on please keep in mind (before you get too far) that you will need some content for your website.

You can create as you go if you wish but you will want to fine tune everything after you do the basics.

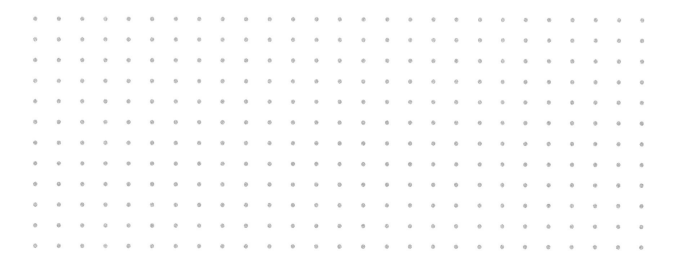

☐   Register Domain & Sign Up For Hosting at www.MyHostLink.com

Once you have found the best name for your business/project the next step is to register your domain and sign up for hosting.

When it comes to registering your domains there are a few options I'd recommend. The first option is HostYak.com which is what I use for about 90% of my domains. The cost with them is under $15/year for a (.com) so it isn't going to break the bank.

If you choose to use HostYak for your domain you will need to purchase your domain before you continue with your hosting.

The second way is to use the "FREE DOMAIN" that you get from signing up for hosting with MyHostLink.com. You can decide to use the FREE DOMAIN & if you do you'll need to jump to the MyHostLink.com section.

HostYak.com

When you land on HostYak.com you will see a domain search box that says "Find your perfect domain name". Simply type in the name you decided on in the previous step and click on search.

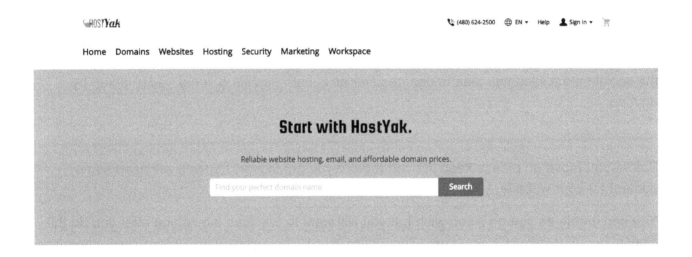

Once you search for your domain and see it's available then just click "Add to Cart"

The next page you land on is the "add-ons" page. The first section you get to is going to be privacy protection. What this does is keep your personal information private from a "Who Is" search. I HIGHLY recommend that you use privacy protection. It's only $1.95/domain per year!

We've added privacy. Here's why.

When you register a domain, your name, address, email address and phone number are automatically published for the world to see. Protect yourself from spam and scams with HostYak Privacy Protection, which replaces your personal information with ours. See Example ?

We highly recommend domain privacy, but it is an **optional** feature.

Select plan

⦿ **Privacy Protection** $1.95/domain per year
View Details ?   ~~$2.99~~

The next option is for hosting, you can host here but I'd recommend you say "No Thanks" and keep going. Moving forward, the last add-on is to add email to your domain. We are going to be using our hosting company to set up our emails so you can go "No Thanks" on this too!

Click Continue with these options.

Before we can check out we need to either Sign in (if you have a HostYak account) or Create Account.

If you need to create an account, simply fill in the blanks and create your account. Then move forward to checkout.

If you have an account, sign in and move forward to checkout.

Now all you need to do is add a payment option and Complete Purchase.

Sometimes the default setting will set your registration period for the domain to 2 years if you wish you can change the registration period to any of the following duration periods (1 Year, 2 Years, 3 Years, 5 Years or 10 Years) as you change the registration duration the privacy length will increase or decrease accordingly.

You now have your domain purchased. Moving forward you will need to get your hosting & once you have your hosting you will need to come back here and change the DNS. Don't worry we are going to cover that in a little bit.

www.MyHostLink.com

When you go to www.MyHostLink.com you will see that you land on the business hosting page.

The best performance package that you can sign up for is "Pro". Click on "Order Now" & then chose the registration duration. It will break down to what it would cost monthly but you are required to pay in advance.

If you wish to select "Launch" or "Power" this will work with either one.

NOTE: The best option is VPS but I'm going to use shared "business" hosting for this tutorial if you want VPS all you need to do is to hover over Web Hosting in the navigation and then VPS Hosting and select Managed VPS Hosting – VPS-1000HA-S will work for most websites. Unfortunately, if you are working with a limited budget, this may be too much. (Don't worry you can upgrade later)

As you move forward with the "Pro" hosting package you'll see the default price is $15.99 per month. Depending on the specials they're running, I've seen them do 43% off like they are doing at the time of me working on this workbook a few times.

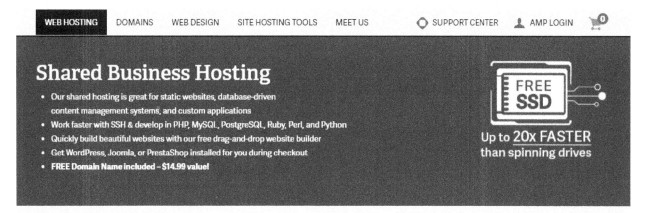

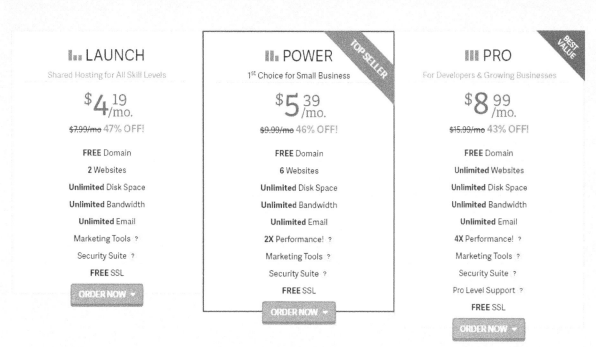

At the time of me doing this you can get 1 year and it will cost about $107.88. (Prices are subject to change.)

Chose your Data Center – If they have availability for multiple servers at the time you sign up you will see multiple options for your data center. If you see the options, just chose the data center closest to you.

Do not install WordPress here. We are going to do this later so we can customize our advanced settings. So keep this section set to "No, Thanks"

Click on "Continue".

Onward to the next step!

But first, just a reminder that we are going to be installing WordPress in a later step and if you want a massive shortcut you can check out the bonus video training at wwww.webdesignwebinar.com

Enter in the domain you want to purchase(if you have not already registered one) on the next page and click search to start the process. Once you see the success message "Great news, thedomainyouwanted.com is available!" click on "Add to Cart" & then click on "Continue"

The next section is for "Domain Privacy Registration". I highly recommend that you keep the privacy registration setting on. For only about $10/year this will keep your information private so that people can't do a "WHOIS" reverse search to find your phone number, email address, mailing address, etc. Click on "Continue"

Once you have done that you will need to create a new account. Under "New Customer" please enter your email address & click continue.

On the next page fill out your information to create your account and complete the purchase. Now click "Continue"

Once you get to the "Review Your Order" page, please be sure to go over all of the information. Then you need to click "I Agree" on the bottom of the page to agree to the purchase & Terms of Service. Then click on "Checkout"

Now you have completed the process to register your domain name and have signed up for hosting. The next thing you need to do is check your email account for an email from InMotion Hosting to set your password & verify your account. Please follow along with those emails in order to complete this step.

☐ Set DNS | Nameservers

If you used the free domain when signing up for your hosting you can skip this step. If you used HostYak then you will need to set your nameservers. This will tell the browsers what host to look at for your website files so when they go to your domain, they see your website.

In order to do this you need to sign in to your HostYak account. Once you sign in you need to get to the "My Products" page and in the "Domains" section, click on Manage All.

The page that will take you to will have all of your domains that you own with HostYak. Click on your URL to get to the domain settings.

Go towards the bottom of the page and click on "Manage DNS"

This is going to take you to the DNS Management page. In the second section you will see the "Nameservers" section.

Click on change and then select custom and enter the nameservers for your hosting account. Most of the time if you are hosting with InMotion your nameservers will be: (ns1.inmotionhosting.com) (ns2.inmotionhosting.com)

If you are not sure what your nameservers are, you can call into your hosting account and they will be able to tell you what they are.

Fill in the nameservers and click on "Save"

☐ Account Management Panel • cPanel

For starters you need to sign into your AMP (Account Management Panel). Which you can do by going inmotionhosting.com and clicking on AMP Login on the top right section of the website. Enter your login information on the next page and login.This is your account Management Panel. **NOTE:** You may see some extra options in the image below but that is because I have the "Reseller Account"

This is going to be your shortcut to your cPanel and how you access your billing portal to upgrade your payments along with viewing other account information.

The main thing you are going to be using here is just logging into cPanel. All you need to do is click on the cPanel logo in the second section.

This will take you to your cPanel. There are a few things here that you will need to know about. Don't worry, I'll cover what you will need to know in order to build your website.

I've cropped the photo on the next page to get each of the categories within the cPanel to fit.

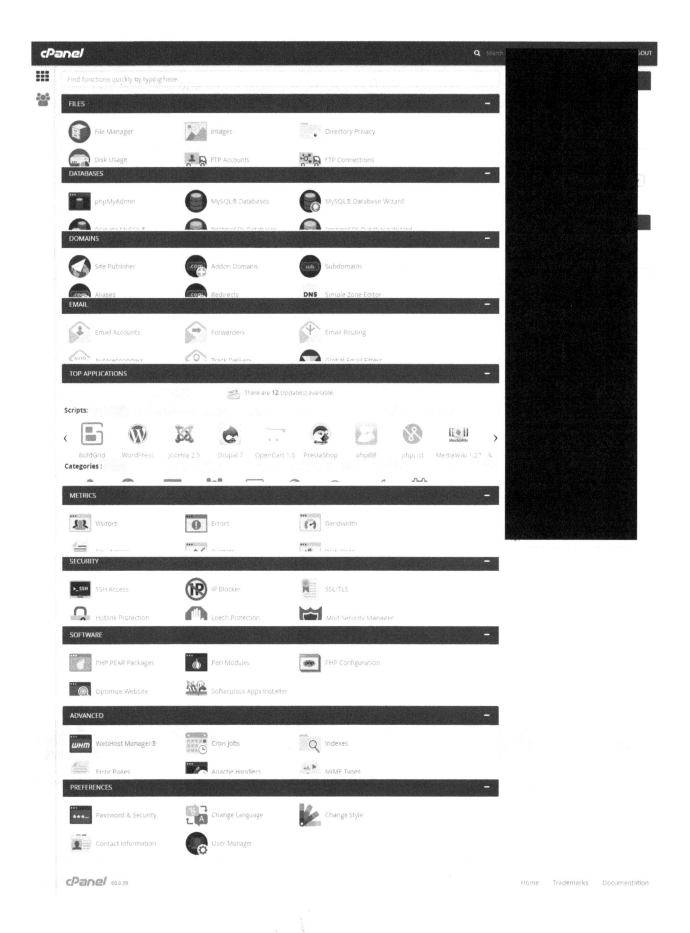

Now it is time to go through the few different options you will need to know.

☐ **Create URL Specific Email**

This is important, because you want to look professional and have all of your emails for your business be you@you.com. Don't worry if you are like me and have been using gmail for years, I'm going to also show you how to send and receive your email via Gmail.

In the fourth section under EMAIL click on "Email Accounts". This is where you create your email address. Enter in what you want your email address to be and your password. Be sure to remember your password. (Use the Password Log) As far as the "Mailbox Quota" I set mine to 250mb because we're having the email go through Gmail so it won't bog down the server for us.

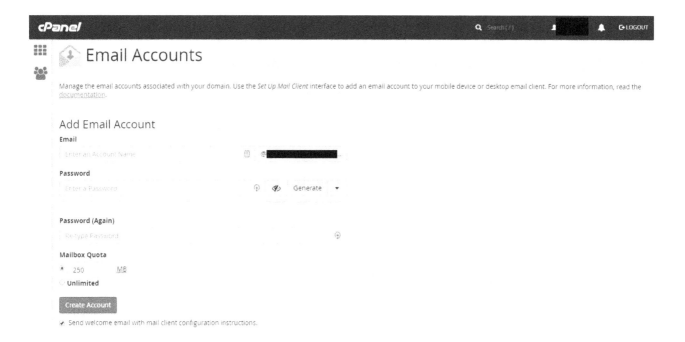

Now that you have the account created scroll down the page and you will see your email with the different actions. This is where you can change the password & quota for this account. You need to open the "More" selection box and select "Access Webmail". You are going to have a small pop up in the upper right hand side of the screen just click on "Got it"

Now you need to click on "Set as Default" under Horde. This will highlight horde. Now click on the horde logo. You will need this open for the next few steps. In a new tab within your browser, go login to Gmail.

On the right hand side of the header there is a gear box. If you click on that it will open up a drop down menu. In that menu you need to click on "Settings". Now that you are in the General Settings you need to click on "Accounts and Import" on the menu across the top of the page.

Send Mail As: You need to click on "Add another email address in the "Send mail as:" section. Enter your Name & Email address then click on Next Step.

Now you need to take the information from that one email inside of your webmail and enter it into the pop up window.

Always be sure to use the Secure SSL/TLS Settings and fill in the following fields:

SMTP Server – Port – Username – Password – Keep SSL selection & click Add Account.

Now you need to verify by checking your Webmail for you@you.com and click on the link in the confirmation email. It may take a few minutes for you to receive it so don't worry.

Once you click on the verify link it will take you to another page with Gmail.

Click on the "Confirm" button and you've verified in order to send mail and now we need to be able to check our mail.

Check Mail From Other Accounts: We're going to follow almost the same steps we used to send mail in this section so we can check mail.

Click on Add a mail account in "Check mail from other accounts:" section. Follow along the prompted steps and enter your email address in the field then click on Next.

The next panel will be to "Import emails from my other account (POP3)

Now it is time to enter in your account information again. (Use Port: 995) Once you finish that all you need to do is click on "Add Account".

That is it! You have finished the first hurdle! Now you can start telling people to email you at your awesome new email address...

_____@_____._____

Go ahead and write it down so you can start to remember it! Don't forget about the password log in the front of the book.

☐   Purchase & Install SSL Certificate • DO NOT SKIP THIS STEP!

I cannot stress enough how important this step is. Before we go through the steps to get our SSL Certificate I want to go over some info with you.

Netscape began using Secure Socket Layer (SSL) in 1994 as a means of sending sensitive data over the web.

Before the introduction of SSL it was difficult to ensure privacy over the web in online transactions & data collection via online forms. There was a general distrust of the ability to conduct online transactions and a fear that an individual's credit card & other personal information could be picked up by a third party and used for unauthorized purchases.

What makes SSL unique is an encryption technique that sends credit card and other personal data through the web. This encryption technique makes the information totally useless to anyone who does not have decoding abilities. If a third party were to intercept the information it would be useless to them.

The use of SSL Digital Certificates also provides a unique level of trust because a certificate verifies the users authenticity. This is an important step in instilling trust in potential customers. Many savvy internet users will avoid websites entirely if they do not use SSL.

Without the proper use of SSL, information such as credit card numbers, third parties with less than positive motivations could obtain passwords and personal identification numbers.

A 128-bit key that is harder to break and typically protects personal account information than the 40-bit key. If your name and address is all that is being protected a 40-bit key may be used; the higher bit the key, the greater level of encryption. Most financial institutions only use 128-but keys for the security of their client's data.

As an online marketer you will likely be asking your visitors for personal data. Don't be surprised if your potential customer determines their willingness to do business with you based on the security of your website. Many customers will look for the SSL symbol and will move along if the don't find it. SSL use can also be recognized by a green padlock symbol in the address bar of your browser window. If the symbol is unlocked then SSL is not in use on the site.

SSL should be enacted on pages requiring a password or might contain personal data most clients would like to keep private. Some sites will place SSL on some pages and forget other pages that are equally as sensitive. For the sake of your personal experience with e commerce you should implement SSL protocol.

Now that we have covered the basics of what an SSL is, let's go buy one & get it set up!

You can purchase your SSL via HostYak by going to: http://www.hostyak.com/products/ssl

The package you need is a Standard SSL. This is going to run you $39.99/year. We will get back to HostYak in a little bit.

In order to activate this we are going to get inside of our InMotion cPanel & under the "Security" panel you need to click on "SSL/TLS".

The first thing we are going to do is to delete all current SSLs that may come with your hosting.

You will see 4 sections. Private Keys, Certificate Signing Requests(This also is refereed to as CSR, Certificates & Install and Manage SSL for your site (HTTPS)

Start by clicking on "Manage SSL sites." under the fourth option.

Under the "Manage Installed SSL Websites" section if you see a certificate you will want to click on "Uninstall"

Once you finish that you need to scroll to the bottom of the page and click on Return to SSL Manager or you can click on the cPanel at the top and go back to the SSL/TLS section again.

The next thing you are going to need to do is to click on "Generate, view, or delete SSL certificate signing requests."

On this page you will need to fill in your information.

Do not worry about the Key section you can skip over that. (Just in case it should say Generate a new 2,048 bit key.)

In the domains section you need to put your domain like this → testedurl.com

Enter your city, state, country, company, email, passphrase(this should be something you can remember – think of this as another password) & a description then click on Generate.

Once you get that you will have your "**Encoded Certificate Signing Request**"

You need to copy the entire thing and past in into a notepad or somewhere where you can keep it and know it's secure:

-----BEGIN CERTIFICATE REQUEST-----
Copy All Of The Crazy Stuff Here Too
-----End CERTIFICATE REQUEST-----

Be sure to **ONLY COPY ENCODED CERTIFICATE SIGNING REQUEST**

Ok, now we need to go back to HostYak. Once you login, you will want to make sure you are on the "My Products" page. Under SSL Certificates, click on "Set up" for the SSL you want to install. (If you only have one then you should only have one.)

That is where you will need to paste your CSR from InMotion. Be sure to agree to the terms and conditions then click on "Request Certificate" This process can take between 10-15 minutes. (It's time for a break! :P)

Now that we've given it some time to issue the certificate, if you should see a screen that has a massive download button.

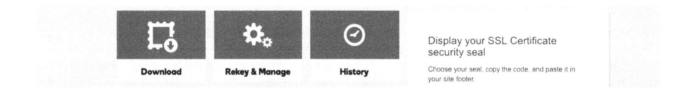

If you click on Download, it will download the certificate that we need to install on InMotion. All you need to do on the next page is to set the server to Apache.

You then will need to "Unzip" the file. (If you are on a PC I recommend using 7-Zip. I've used it for a few months and love it. PS. It is FREE!) (If you are on a mac you should be able to double click on the zip file to unzip it.)

When you unzip the file it will have a file that is a .crt inside of the folder. We are going to use this file next so be sure to have it in a location you can find on your computer.

Now, if you go back in your InMotion cPanel and go back to the SSL/TLS section you need to click on "Generate, view, upload, or delete SSL certificates." under "Certificates (CRT)"

The next thing that we're going to is delete the "- Self Signed -"certificates that are on your server. This is easy, all you need to do (if you have a "- Self Signed -" certificate) is click on delete. It will take you to another page asking if you are sure ... click delete again.

If you go back to the SSL Certificates (CRT) page you will need to click on "Choose File" and then fill out your description and click on Upload Certificate.

Once you do that you should get a success message:

"The certificate for the domain "yourwebsitename.com" has been saved.

Moving forward everything that you do with your website should be done via https://

If you don't know what that means and you are just following along, don't worry. Just keep following the steps and you will be fine.

Our brains work in their own way, so if you need to take some notes before we go any further, this is for you.

☐   Install WordPress

For this step you are going to need to Login to your "AMP" (Account Management Panel) for InMotion Hosting.

In the second panel down you should see the cPanel logo all you need to do is click on that to get into your cPanel.

NOTE: This step and the next few may take a while. If you want a shortcut to take that will skip strait to designing your site in the next 10 minutes or so, you can get the FREE VIDEO TRAINING that will go along with this book to design your website. Just visit WebDesignWebinar.com & use referral code: WB310

Once in your cPanel, you will need to go down to the "Top Applications" panel and click on the WordPress logo. This will take you to the install WordPress page.

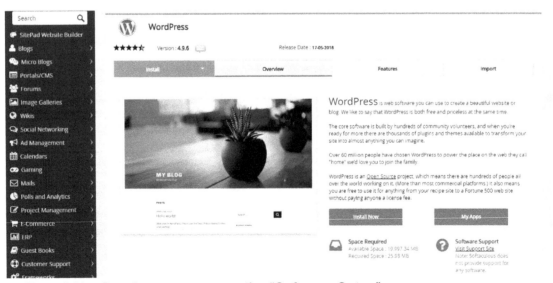

Click on "Install Now" and now you are on the "Software Setup" page.

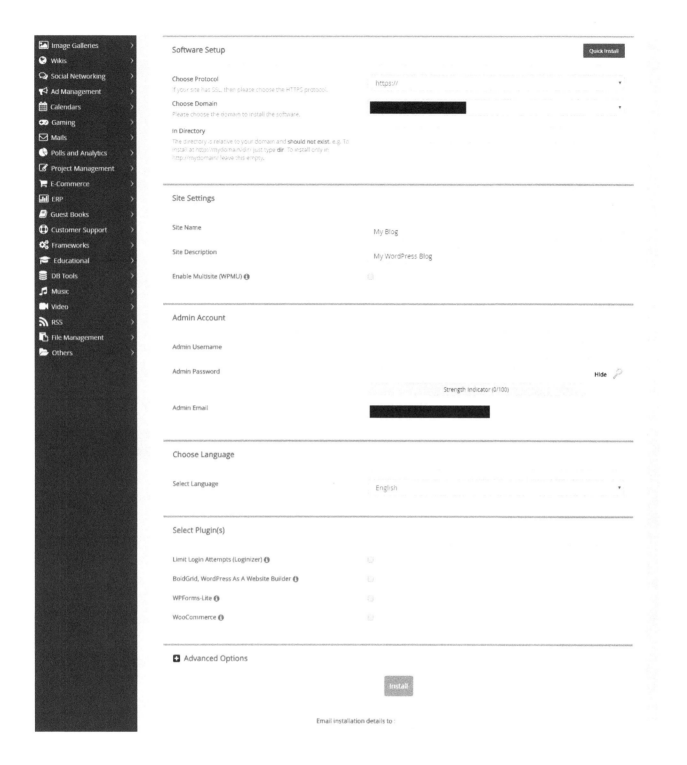

Choose the right protocol. This is very important to ensure that your website is secure.

Choose your domain. If you are using a larger plan from InMotion Hosting you may have added some "Add On Domains" in which case you will have multiple domains to choose from. If not then just make sure your domain is selected.

The next section is for your "Directory", you will need to keep this empty. This will install WordPress on your actual domain instead of yourdomain.com/blog

In the "Site Settings" panel simply fill out your Site Name & Site Description.

Leave the "Enable Multisite (WPMU)" checkbox unchecked

The "Admin Account" panel is going to be used to create your "User Account". So fill in a username & password. We are going to be creating your actual user account later so for now just use the info below.

Username: start

Password: #delete

Un-check selected plugins (We're going to cover plugins later)

Now, the next section "Advanced Options" is going to be very important so I need you to pay attention!!

Touch Nothing! :)

The next thing you need to do is simply click on "Install" and you have now successfully installed WordPress on your domain.

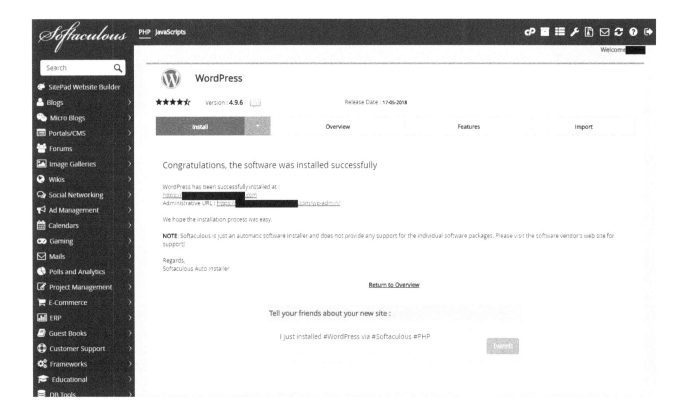

Congratulations! You Have Successfully Installed The WordPress Software On Your Site!

Unfortunately, we are far from being finished. Moving forward there are some more boring steps, but don't worry. We are going to be into the design part of our website project soon enough.

☐ Login to WordPress Dashboard & Create New User

Once you have installed WordPress you can login to your website by going to yourwebsite.com/wp-admin. This will take you to the login page.

Admin URL: _____/wp-admin

If you followed along with the tutorial it should be: Username: start | Password: #delete • Now, you should be inside of your Dashboard.

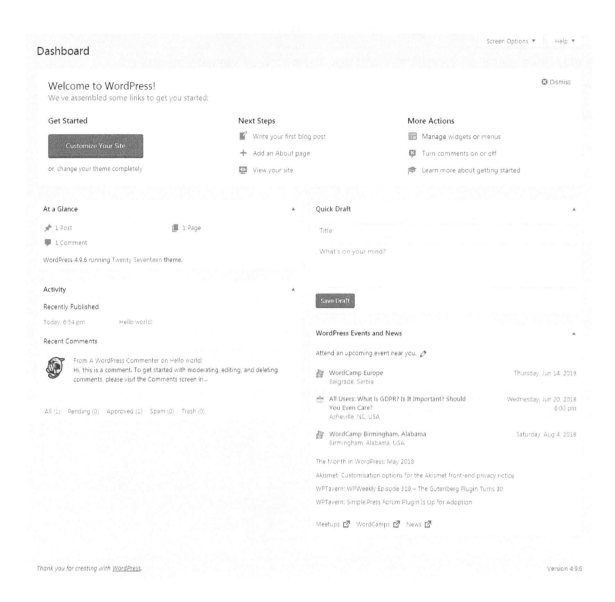

Dashboard

Welcome to WordPress!
We've assembled some links to get you started:

Get Started

Customize Your Site

or, change your theme completely

Next Steps

✏ Write your first blog post
✚ Add an About page
🖥 View your site

More Actions

🖽 Manage widgets or menus
🚫 Turn comments on or off
📢 Learn more about getting started

At a Glance

📌 1 Post   📄 1 Page
💬 1 Comment

WordPress 4.9.6 running Twenty Seventeen theme.

Activity

Recently Published

Today, 6:54 pm   Hello world!

Recent Comments

From A WordPress Commenter on Hello world!
Hi, this is a comment. To get started with moderating, editing, and deleting comments, please visit the Comments screen in...

All (1)   Pending (0)   Approved (1)   Spam (0)   Trash (0)

Quick Draft

Title

What's on your mind?

Save Draft

WordPress Events and News

Attend an upcoming event near you. ✏

🏕 WordCamp Europe   Thursday, Jun 14, 2018
   Belgrade, Serbia

📅 All Users: What Is GDPR? Is It Important? Should   Wednesday, Jun 20, 2018
   You Even Care?   6:00 pm
   Asheville, NC, USA

🏕 WordCamp Birmingham, Alabama   Saturday, Aug 4, 2018
   Birmingham, Alabama, USA

The Month in WordPress: May 2018

Akismet: Customisation options for the Akismet front-end privacy notice

WPTavern: WPWeekly Episode 319 – The Gutenberg Plugin Turns 30

WPTavern: Simple:Press Forum Plugin Is Up for Adoption

Meetups 🗗   WordCamps 🗗   News 🗗

Thank you for creating with WordPress.

Version 4.9.6

Screen Options ▼   Help ▼

❌ Dismiss

You can go ahead and "Dismiss" (or click on the X) to close the "Welcome to WordPress" section.

The next step is very important. The reason we are doing this separately and not earlier when we installed WordPress is because you need to get all the information filled out and not skip anything.

Go down on the left sidebar and go to Users > Add New

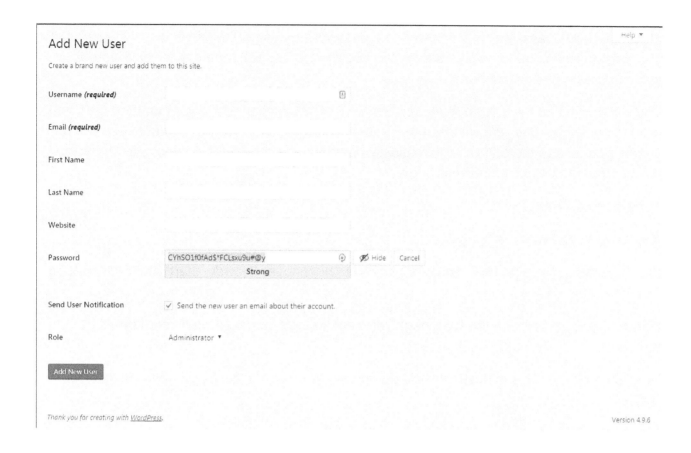

Username: This needs to be around 6-10 characters and needs to be original. DO NOT USE "ADMIN", "WEBMASTER" or anything else like that. Feel free to use your name or nickname.

Email: Put in a valid email address. Your new email address we created earlier would be

Fill out your First Name & Last Name.

In the "Website" section you need to include the full link so it should look something like this (https://yourwebsitename.com)

Password: This is a touchy subject. I know how much you may want to create a password that you can remember, but that could cost you in the end. Click on the "Show password" button to edit & show your password.

I'd recommend you create a password that is 10-15 characters long that includes lowercase (a,b,c), uppercase (A, B, C), numbers (1,2,3) & special characters (!, @, #).

I highly recommend that you use the "Password Generator" and just remember to WRITE IT DOWN! OR... Find a creative way to remember it!

Username: _____

Password: _____

Check the box to "Send User Notification" • Then set the "Role" to "Administrator"

Then click on "Add New User" & that is it!

If you don't like the fact of writing down your passwords you can use something like LastPass (http://litl.me/lastpass) which is an awesome password manager that is secure. It stores all of your passwords on an encrypted server that you can access with one master password that you can create and remember.

You will notice that there is an Avatar or "Profile Picture" section within your user profile if you want to customize this, you will need to create a WordPress.com & gravatar.com account and update your image there. It will automatically update everywhere else on your site and when you comment on other WordPress sites.

IMPORTANT NOTE

You need to do two more things.

First is in the upper right hand corner you need to hover over "Howdy, start" and click on "Log Out".

Now that you are back on the login page you need to login with your new username & password.

Next thing on the list is to delete the old username. You can do this by going to Users > All Users

Hover over the old user "start" and click on "Delete"

On the next page you need to check "Delete all content." and then click on "Confirm Deletion"

This will automatically get rid of all default content by the initial installation of WordPress. The only thing you need to do now is to go into the "Trash" and permanently delete all trash. You can do that by starting with "All Posts" at the top of that page you will see "Trash (X)" Click on the top box to select all then in the "Bulk Actions" drop down box, simply select "Delete Permanently" and then click on the "Apply" button.

Repeat this step for "Pages".

☐ Install GeneratePress WordPress Theme

Installing your WordPress theme is very easy. Once you login you go to install your theme by ..

Dashboard > Appearance > Theme > Add New

Once your are on the Add New WordPress Theme Page all you need to do is search for your desired theme.

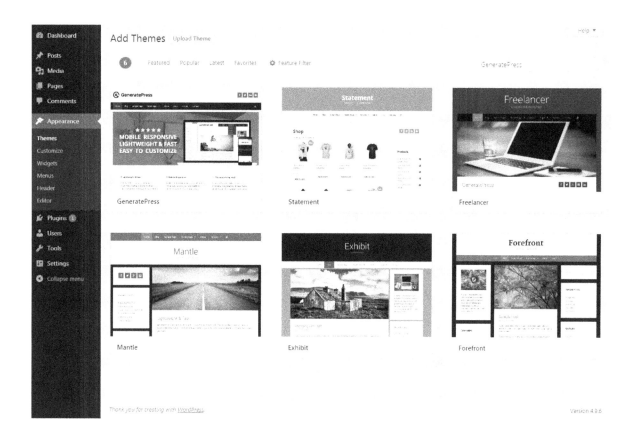

GeneratePress is the WordPress Theme we are going to be using. Once you Search for the theme, simply install & activate. When you hover over the theme thumbnail you will see a "Preview" (Don't worry about this, we are going to customize the entire site so this won't matter) and then you will see an "Install" button. Click on "Install" and once it installs that same button will turn into an "Activate" button. Click on "Activate". That is it!

Now, you need to delete all of the other default WordPress themes.

From the "Themes" page, hover over the other themes and click on "Theme Details" then in the bottom right corner of the theme popup click on "Delete"

You will get a popup asking for you to confirm. Click "OK". Repeat until GeneratePress is the only theme left.

☐ Install, Activate & Setup WordPress Plugins

Before we install any plugins you need to delete the default plugins. Visit Plugins > Installed Plugins & on that page you can select them by checking the box next to the word Plugin to "Select All" then in the drop down "Bulk Actions" box, select Delete. Then click "Apply". It will bring up a "pop up" asking if you are sure … go ahead and agree to delete the plugins.

This first plugin we're going to install will help us "Bulk Install" all of the needed plugins.

NOTE: This is a shortcut. If you would like to skip this step and do the installations one at a time, then by all means, go ahead. (Seriously, I'd recommend that you use the shortcut and save yourself about 10-15 minutes.)

Start by installing WP Favs – Plugin Manager by searching for the plugin via:

Dashboard > Plugins > Add New

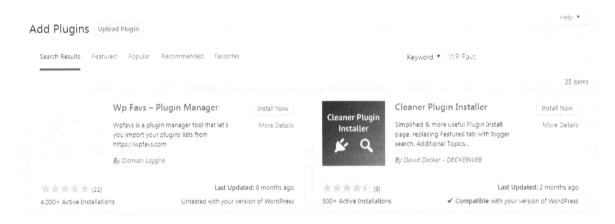

Install & Activate by clicking on "Install Now" then "Activate" once it installs. Once the plugin is "Active" go to the settings via: Dashboard > Tools > WP Favs

Insert the Quick Key & click on "Quick Load" Quick Key (QK):

DwsDsjH5N92QXgHwNQWoKovAWHo0du

Once you have clicked on Quick Load you will want to click on "Run this List".

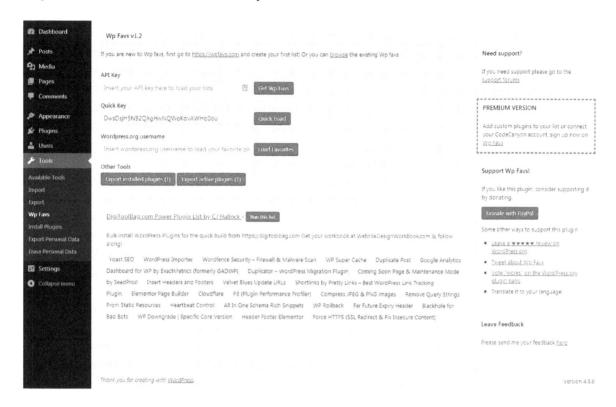

This will take you to our magic list of WordPress Plugins. These are the recommended plugins for this tutorial. (Image has been cropped to save space)

Click on the drop down over the plugins labeled "Bulk Options" and then select "Install" Check the first box (to the right of Plugin column label) to Select All Plugins.

Then Click Apply to install all plugins.

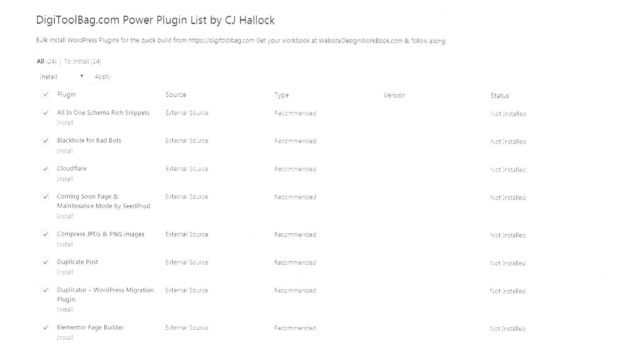

After it installs you may see some warnings from the install process, don't worry those shouldn't be a problem. At the bottom of the page you will see a success message:

All Installations have been completed.

Click on "Return to WP Favs Installer", underneath that message, and move onto the next task. If you wish to do this manually you can be installing and activating each plugin one by one.

Use your judgment in using the recommended plugins. Only you know what you are doing and what you need. The plugins you are going to Activate will depend on what you will need for your website.

To "Activate" your plugins you need to check the box next to the plugins you wish to use and once all your plugins are checked in the drop down menu (Bulk Actions) select "Activate" and "Apply". This will "Activate" all of your desired plugins.

> The following plugins were activated successfully: All In One Schema Rich Snippets, Blackhole for Bad Bots, Cloudflare, Coming Soon Page & Maintenance Mode by SeedProd, Compress JPEG & PNG images, Duplicate Post, Duplicator – WordPress Migration Plugin, Elementor Page Builder, Far Future Expiry Header, Force HTTPS (SSL Redirect & Fix Insecure Content), Google Analytics Dashboard for WP by ExactMetrics (formerly GADWP), Header Footer Elementor, Heartbeat Control, Insert Headers and Footers, P3 (Plugin Performance Profiler), Remove Query Strings From Static Resources, Shortlinks by Pretty Links – Best WordPress Link Tracking Plugin, Velvet Blues Update URLs, WP Downgrade | Specific Core Version, WP Rollback, WP Super Cache, WordPress Importer, Wordfence Security – Firewall & Malware Scan and Yoast SEO.

We are not going to be using all plugins, all of the time so we will be deactivating a few. Also, feel free to close any of the warning messages you see within your dashboard. The recommended plugins for EVERY installation of WordPress are:

All In One Scheme Rich Snippets – This amazing plugin gives the power to the blog author to control the rich snippets to be shown by the search engines. There are 9 "Rich Snippets" that you can utilize. Go deeper into this via DigiToolBag.com/rich-snippets & learn what rich snippets are & how to use them.

- Item Review – This is great for a review of a product that you use for your business.

- Event – This works great for open houses or other events for your business.

- People – If you run an office where you want to showcase employees, use this.

- Product – This would be great for a detailed page that leads to a shopping cart.

- Recipe - Yes, recipes! :P

- Software Application – Might not use this unless your in the tech industry.

- Video- This works for blog posts with a supporting video embedded.

- Article – This isn't for "Blog Posts" but if you are doing a write up/news, this is it!

- Service – This is perfect for your service specific pages. (Painting, Plumbing, etc.)

Blackhole for Bad Bots – This puts all bots in a "Black Hole" so they don't use your server's resources. Once active, the plugin does all the hard work. No settings needed here.

Cloudflare – This is a plugin that works with the platform "Cloudflare" and speeds up your loading time and increases your security for your WordPress website.

Coming Soon Page & Maintenance Mode by SeedProd – This is one of my favorite coming soon plugins and is self proclaimed "The #1 Coming Soon Page, Under Construction & Maintenance Mode plugin for WordPress."

Compress JPEG & PNG images – This is a plugin that helps you optimize your images for mobile & page speed within your media library.

Duplicate Post – This is not a "must install plugin" but it does help if you have template style blog posts to be able to just create a "clone" of a specific page and start with it as a new draft.

Duplicator – This amazing "FREE" website helps migrate and backup a copy of your website files and database and helps you duplicate or move your websites very easy. There is a bonus video training at www.webdesignwebinar.com that will show you how I use this plugin to build professional websites in under an hour.

Elementor "Page Builder" – This is the WYSIWYG (What You See Is What You Get) page builder we are going to use to build/design your website. For this tutorial I'm also going to be using the "**Elementor Pro**" paid version. It isn't a must but it does give you a lot more options when it comes to designing your pages.

View more info at: DigiToolBag.com/elementor

Elementor Pro – Like I said before you can continue without this plugin but at only $49 you will see the value in the paid version Buy the plugin here → DigiToolBag.com/buyelementor. You will have to upload the plugin(See Bonus Chapter)

Far Future Expiry Header – This assists in your page load speed. Go to Settings > FarFutureExpiry & check to Enable Far Future Expiration. Set the Number of Days to 7 and click all file types. Click to Enable Gzip Compression & click on "Save"

Force HTTPS (SSL Redirect & Fix Insecure Content) – When it comes to making your site secure with SSL encryption this plugin helps tell the browsers to load your site through the encryption for everything. If you followed the SSL steps earlier all you need to do is keep this active. That is it!

Google Analytics Dashboard for WP (GADWP) – This displays Google Analytics reports and real-time statistics in your "Dashboard." It also automatically inserts the tracking code inside of every page on your website.

Heartbeat Control – It's hard to explain but this completely controls the WordPress heartbeat which basically means … it speeds your website up.

Insert Headers and Footers – This is for putting code in your headers or footers. If you are using Google Analytics or something that needs "code" in the <head> or above the </body> section this is how you do that. Go to Settings > Insert Headers and Footers.

Pretty Links – This is like bit.ly for your website. For example if I want to create a short-link for my new YouTube channel, instead of it being

https://www.youtube.com/channel/xxxxxxxxxxxxxxxxxxxxxxxxxxx)

I can use Shortlinks and make it look like this: **http://testedurl.com/yt**

Remove Query Strings From Static Resources – This helps your load speed. No settings for this plugin.

Wordfence Security – Firewall & Malware Scan - Wordfence includes an endpoint firewall and malware scanner that were built from the ground up to protect WordPress. Our Threat Defense Feed arms Wordfence with the newest firewall rules, malware signatures and malicious IP addresses it needs to keep your website safe. Rounded out by a suite of additional features, Wordfence is the most comprehensive WordPress security solution available.

WP Super Cache – This helps with browser caching (page load speed) Go to Settings > WP Super Cache

You are going to click on the "Advanced" tab & be sure that the following boxes are checked:

Enable Caching

Simple (Recommended)

Don't cache pages for known users. (Recommended)

Compress pages so they're served more quickly to visitors. (Recommended)

Cache rebuild. Serve a supercache file to anonymous users while a new file is being generated. (Recommended)

304 Not Modified browser caching. Indicate when a page has not been modified since it was last requested. (Recommended)

Clear all cache files when a post or page is published or updated.

Extra homepage checks. (Very occasionally stops homepage caching) (Recommended)

At the bottom of this section, click "Update Status" and you are done!

Yoast SEO – This is the best SEO plugin on the market. The settings for the plugin itself is decent for now without having to customize. The power of this plugin will come when using it while creating posts & pages within WordPress.

☐ How to Upload a WordPress Plugin (& Activate Elementor Pro License)

Once you have the plugin file (.zip) you need to go to Plugins> Add New. Once you are on the install plugins page you will see a button at the top of the page that says "Upload Plugin". If you click on that button you will start the process.

The first thing you need to do is to click on "Choose File" and select the plugin file on your computer. Once you have the file selected, simply click on "Install Now".

This will automatically take care of installing the plugin, leaving the only thing for you to do is to "Activate Plugin" by clicking on that button.

Once Elementor Pro Plugin is Active, you will see a banner in the top of your website

If you click on the Activate License button this will take you to the activation page. This is where you will put in your license key. If you do not know how to gain access to your Elementor License key you can sign into Elementor.com & from your Elementor account you will see the "Download Plugin" to download your copy as well as your License Key.

Simply copy your license and paste it into WordPress & click on "Activate"

☐   Permalink Structure

This step is very important. Luckily, it is very easy. Before I go into the changes I just want to let you know the answer to the question you might be thinking right now...

What is a Permalink?

Basically it is a link to a specific page on your website.

per·ma·link
/ˈpərməˌliNGk/ ◀))

noun
plural noun: **permalinks**

    a permanent static hyperlink to a particular web page or entry in a blog.

You need to go under "Settings" and click on "Permalinks" Then you need to select "Post Name" and click on "Save Changes" … That is it! :) It may seem like a small step but you will appreciate this as we move forward building our website.

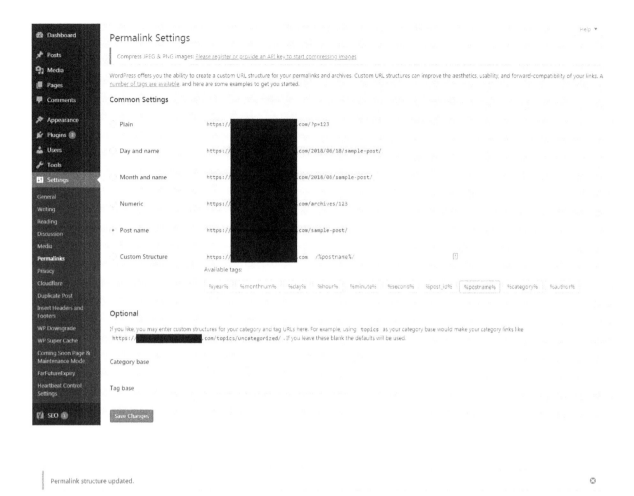

Permalink structure updated.

☐   Create Fundamental Pages

Keep in mind that this is just the "Create" step. We are going to go back and add content as well as design the pages later. For now you are just going to create the pages and set the proper settings.

In your "Dashboard" you want to hover over "Pages" in the left sidebar and click on "Add New". Once the draft page is open you need to do the following.

Title – fill in the title for this page (IE, Contact, About, Services)

Permalink – This should fill in automatically. If not just put the same as the title. If you have a title like "About Us" just use yourdomain.com/about … keep it simple for your visitors.

Layout – There are a few things that we will do here. In the "Sidebars" section you will want to be sure that "Content (no sidebars)" is selected. Then under the "Disable Elements" section you will want to check "Content Title".

Then Publish!

Here are the pages you should create (Use your own judgment and create only what you need):

Home • About • Blog * • Services • Contact

* For the "Blog" page you will be just putting in the "Title" and publishing.

I do not know your business so you may have other pages you want to create or you may not ever plan on blogging from this site in which case you wouldn't create the blog page.

Please seek legal advice for the legal pages you may need on your website. I personally have three legal pages that go on most of my websites. You can find free templates online but there is no guarantee until you have legal council look over the terminology. **For legal pages do not disable the Content Title.

Terms & Conditions – This is a strong page that is basically what the people agree to when using your website. (It's a bit more complicated than that but that is why I'm not a lawyer.)

Privacy Policy – With the new GDPR laws going into effect recently, there are a lot of things you will need to include in this ESPECIALLY if you do any business in the EU.

Earnings Disclaimer – Because I do a lot of affiliate marketing and get paid based on recommendations that I make, I always have an earnings disclaimer. This is to inform your visitors that you will be paid if they take action on your recommendations or anything like that. Please look up all laws based on your industry with the Federal Trade Commission to ensure that you follow all laws pertaining to your specific needs.

☐ Customize WordPress Settings

This is where you will begin getting your content in play to get started with designing your website. Before we complete this section you will need to have a color palette in mind as well as your logo and site icon.

I wanted to try and keep this checklist short but this section can't be any shorter so this is what you need to do.

<u>Don't Forget To Optimize All Media You Upload To Your Library**</u>**

Optimizing your media/images doesn't have to be hard. You can upload them in batches of 20 to TinyPNG.com and have that awesome site optimize everything for you. The reason for doing this is to make sure the images are sized appropriate so that it doesn't take 20-30 seconds to load your website.

The first thing your going to do is hover over "Appearance" and click on "**Customize**".

Customize Settings

Site Identity – This is one of the most important parts of this process. This is where you will be giving your website a name, tagline, and uploading your website logo & icon.

Set your "Site Title" as the name of your business or what you are going to be building your website about. Check the box to "Hide Site Title"

In the next section you will type in your "Tagline" It doesn't have to be final, you can change this later if you need to. So if you don't have a "tagline" in mind just come up with something for now that tells visitors what you do. IE. The best X Company in Y city and surrounding areas. Check the box to "Hide Site Tagline"

The next section is for your logo. The suggested image dimensions is 350px X 70px but you can use different different sizes if you want. If you chose to use different dimensions you will just "Skip Cropping" when uploading your image. After you upload your image you will see a "Retina Logo" section appear. The Retina Logo is the same logo but twice the size. So if you used the suggested dimensions for your regular logo, the retina logo should be 700px X 140px.

Last but not least, upload your "Site Icon". (Website Icon should be 512px x 512px) This is going to be used as the "Favicon" for your website, which is the icon that displays in the tab within your browser when people visit your website.

Don't forget the Alt Text and the Description when you upload images to your website as well as run them through TinyPNG.com to be sure to optimize your images for page speed.

Click "Publish" and once it is saved go back to the main customize tab by clicking the left facing arrow underneath the save button.

The next section is "Layout". There is only one section that we are going to be changing. That is the "Footer" Section. Inside of the "Footer Widgets" drop down box, select "0" and publish. Now, you should be good to go. Return to the Customizer menu.

The next phase is your "Colors" - You can change colors as you design your page but if you want to keep to a specific color pallet you can set your colors here. Just be sure to save your settings.

Typography is the next section. This is where you will set what your preferred font is going to be. If you are not sure what font you want to use you can browse through the Google Font Library by going to Fonts.Google.com.

The "General" section/tab should have the "Cache Dynamic CSS" check box, checked.

Menus is the next section & in this section we are going to create 2 menus

In this section click on Create New Menu

Create Main Menu - Create a name for this menu "Main Menu" will work. Then underneath that section check the "Primary Menu" box & click next.

This is going to be the menu that is displayed in your header. I have some example pages listed below but remember what you are building your website for and add any needed pages.

Add the following pages by clicking on "+Add Items"

- Home (Custom Link)

- About

- Contact

- Blog

Click/Hold & Drag to reorder if desired.

Publish & Continue. Now go back to the "Menus" tab and create another menu

Create Footer Menu – This is going to display the "Legal" pages.

Follow the same steps as before but name this menu "Footer" and check the "Footer" box & click "Next". These pages are recommended so you may need to either reach out to a lawyer friend to get help writing these or look up some of the free generators online. I can make some recommendations but it is not something (because I'm not a lawyer) that I feel good about recommending. So do your own research.

Add the following pages by clicking on "+Add Items"

- Terms of Use Agreement

- Privacy Policy

- Earnings Disclaimer (If Needed)

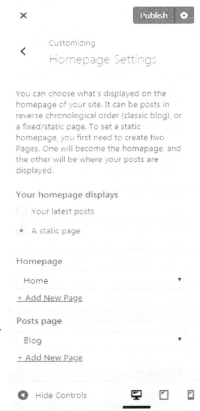

Click/Hold & Drag to reorder if desired.

Publish & Continue

Widgets – This section we are not going to be covering until we start blogging so you can skip it for now. The widget area we will be using isn't listed in this section.

Homepage Settings – This is where we tell WordPress what our home page is going to be and what page our Blog is going to be.

Click on the circle for "A static page"

In the "Homepage" drop down, select "Home" (or whatever you have for your home page)

In the Posts Page drop down, select "Blog".

Now is a GREAT time to "Publish" and save your work.

Additional CSS -(Coding) ... Unless you know what you are doing & understand code, _**DO NOT TOUCH THIS SECTION**_.

☐   Start Designing Your Website

This is going to be where you can let your creative light shine! We are going to use an awesome visual designer plugin called Elementor. You can do all of this with the free version that you should have already installed. If you would like to have other options then feel free to use the Elementor Pro plugin.

You can buy a copy of it for $49 here: WebsiteDesignToolBox.com/elementor

If you aren't creative and don't have an idea on how your website should look, don't worry Elementor has you covered with FREE templates for everything you need. Follow along as we sketch out our designs for our website.

☐   Plan Your Header

When it comes to your header, there are a few things that are AN ABSOLUTE MUST!

- Logo

- Navigational Menu

- Social Media Links

- Call-To-Action

This can be done very easily. There is a section below for your own design in segments. Before we get started I need you to understand that your header will either help or hurt your conversion from website visitor to potential customer. So keep your customers in mind and think like your visitors when designing your header. My #1 tip is to keep it simple and easy to use/navigate.

You should also keep in mind that the only think you NEED is your logo & navigation. So you can chose to not have a "Top Bar".

Top Bar – This is normally where I would put things like social media icons that link out to my social media profiles, phone number, a call-to-action button or maybe an address if you have a physical location. You also want to think about if you want a specific background & font color.

Think about your Top Bar. Use the different templates based on if you want one, two or three columns in your header & feel free to get a little creative.

Call Us Today! (555) 555-5555

Social Media Icons	Contact Us Today → CLICK HERE

Social Media Icons	(555) 555-5555	Contact Us Today → CLICK HERE

Header Hero Section – This is where you will normally have your logo & website navigation. Remember you want to keep it simple so I wouldn't do much more than those two things. If so it should be something that is clean and easy to understand/use.

Use the templates below to think about how you want your website header to look.

Logo	Navigational Menu

Social Media Icons	Logo	Navigational Menu

Logo	Navigational Menu	(555) 555-5555

Now is time to put your thoughts together on paper. Please use a pencil so you can make changes you need until you finalize what you are wanting. I have a few below just in case if you make a mistake and can't erase it. If you don't want to use a top bar just leave it empty.

Top Bar Content Goes Here

Hero Header Content Goes Here

Top Bar Content Goes Here

Hero Header Content Goes Here

Top Bar Content Goes Here

Hero Header Content Goes Here

☐   Plan Your Footer

Your footer is normally something that few people will look at but when they are looking for specific information, a lot of people will go strait to the footer for it. Here are some examples of things you can put into your footer.

- Legal Pages (Privacy Policy, Terms & Conditions, Disclaimer, etc)

- Logo

- Stand Alone Disclaimer

- Search Box

- ©Copyright Information

- Contact/N.A.P. Information (Name, Address, Phone Number)

- Recommended Links

- Social Media Links

- Hours Of Operation

Here are a few examples of footers and a blank template to design your footer.

©20XX Copyright Company Name	Logo	Legal Pages

©20XX Copyright Company Name		Legal Pages

Company Name	Legal Pages	©20XX Copyright Company Name
123 Street, Drive	Privacy Policy	www.WebsiteName.com
City, State 00000	Terms & Conditions	name@websitename.com

Sketch out your footer here:

☐ Design Your Header/Footer with Elementor

Now that you know how you are wanting your header and footer to look you can design them. In order to do that you need to hover over Elementor in the sidebar and click on "My Templates".

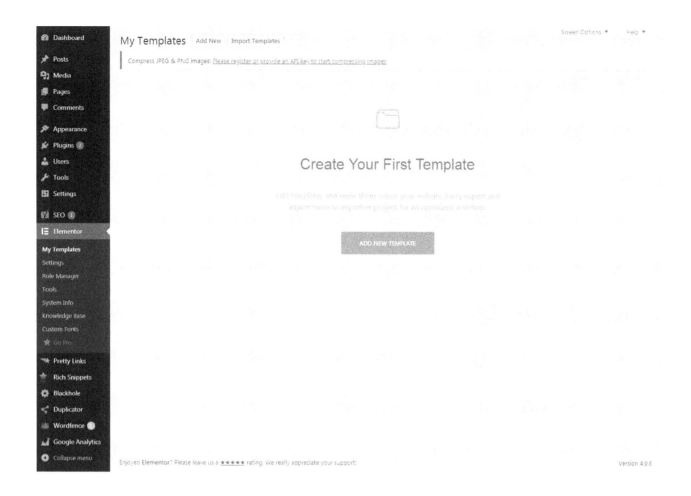

Click on "Add New Template"

In the drop down box select "Header" then give the template a name... "header" works fine! :)

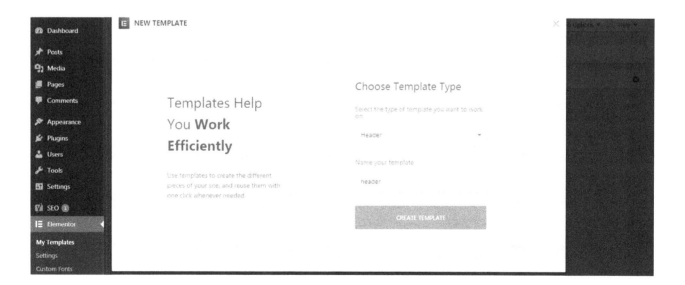

Now the fun begins.

You will see the templates for headers that comes with Elementor Pro. It does offer one header for the free version but you are limited with what you can do with the menus.

Feel free to select the closest header to what you would like your header to look like.

When you select the template you want to move forward with, hover over that template and click on "Insert".

You may want to do some customization to the template you chose and that is fine but for right now we are going to move forward with the footer template.

Don't worry I'm going to cover the inner workings of the Elementor Page Builder plugin in a bonus section later on.

Click on Publish. Now you need to add a condition, which basically tells Elementor where this header will be displayed.

If you click on "Add Condition" the default will "Include" + "Entire Site" which is what we need. So click on Publish again.

Now, repeat this step with the "Footer"

This time, when you get to the "My Templates" page you will click on the "Footer" tab in order to move forward.

The process will work the same here as it did for the header.

☐ Designing Your Website Pages

This is a section that could be 500 pages by itself. There are a lot of different things you may want to have on your pages. I recommend that you think about who your visitor is and what they need to see in order to become a customer/client. In doing that you can open up the page (Edit) you are designing and click on "Edit with Elementor"

If you feel comfortable with knowing what you want your site to look like you can start by using the "Add New Section" selection and start adding elements and designing your pages. But, if you feel you would like to have a little bit of help for ideas and layouts then you can select "Add Template". While this will show a decent collection of templates you will notice some of them have "Pro" in the upper right hand corner. Those templates cannot be used unless you have Elementor Pro.

So if you do not have Elementor Pro you can continue with the free templates and moving forward all you need to do if you find a template you like is just click on "Insert" and from there you are just replacing the content that comes with the template with your own.

NOTE: While the images used with these templates are public domain, they are not optimized for page speed. So you should use your own photos in the templates and keep in mind that if you don't have images to use, you want to be sure you have the legal rights to use any image that you want on your website along with any images you want to post for marketing on social media sites and stuff like that. You can get free public domain images that you can use for commercial use at sites like StockVault.net, UnSplash.com, and Pexels.com.

Now, we are going to go over a few different pages that, in my opinion, should be on every website as well as what each of them should have.

You also have some pages to draw out your ideas so please use them.

Home Page

When it comes to your home page, it is king! (or queen) Most of the traffic to your website will be funneled through your home page. So you need to make sure it is clear in what you do along with where you want your visitors to go. Here are some things you should have on your home page.

- Headline – A successful website should always have a clear and simple "headline" to tell it's visitors what it is about and it should be at the top of the website or "Above the Fold" which basically means they can see it without having to scroll.

- Sub-Headline – This is simply a supportive headline that offers a brief description of what you do and/or offer.

- Primary Call-to-Action (CTA) – This is why you are building a website! You want to have something that tells people what to do in order to do business with you. (IE. Call Us For A Free Estimate, Schedule A Consultation)Your Primary CTA should be "Above The Fold" Keep in mind you may want to have 2-3 supportive CTA's spread throughout the rest of your page as well.

- Benefits – What you do is important but if your visitors don't know the benefits of working with you then they are likely to do business with someone else.

- Social Proof – People do business with people they know, like, and trust. If they do not know, like or trust you yet, a testimonial is a great way to show that you can be trusted and helps you close the gap on people wanting to know and eventually liking you. Let's hope :)

- Bonus Offer Opt-In – This is the hardest thing because it means more work. But having a bonus/download for your visitors will show that you know what you are talking about and can be looked at as the expert in your field. This can be an exclusive video (that is only available to people who opt-in) or an e-book/report/white-paper that covers questions they may have. (IE: What Every Home Owner Should Know About Home Owners Insurance, 21 Health Benefits Of Smoothies, 5 Things Everyone Should Know Before Buying Their Next Car.)

- Features – In support to the Benefits it is helpful to give people more of an understanding of what's provided by using your products and/or services.

- Industry Resources – There is a good chance that a first time visitor to your website isn't ready to do business with you yet. Offering a link to a resource page or even a small resource section on your home page where they can learn more, will help you establish your credibility as the go-to expert and thought leader in your industry.

- Supportive Images/Visuals – All images/videos/icons should be supportive of the content on the page. Remember that these need to be optimized for page speed (TinyPNG.com) as well as for SEO (Don't forget to fill in Alt Tag & Description for your images)

Sketch Out Your Home Page Design – You can work on the actual written content later...

About Page

When it comes to your about page, this is where people get to know not only about your business but also about the people who run it.

This is going to be similar to the home page because you should include things like a good "headline", 1-2 "CTAs", "benefits" and "social proof" you should also include a few other things like:

- Mission Statement – This is important to have for two reasons. The first is because whether you believe it or not, having your mission statement holds you accountable to it and the second reason is because it tells your visitor what you are doing this for.

- Vision Statement – Similar to the "Mission Statement" this is important because it let's your visitors know that your vision for a successful future means you aren't going away any time soon.

- Your Story – Don't hold back when writing the story of your business. If you remember I said earlier in the social proof section for the home page, people do business with people they know like and trust. Sharing your story, struggle and all, will help people relate to you and want to do business with you! Yes, I did say to include the struggle. People are use to seeing "My Business Is Great" but when you open up and share the real story including when you had to get a title loan on your car to pay for the supplies to get started it makes the business look more like a person instead of a machine that would just look at them as a number.

You will also need to emphasize your Unique Selling Proposition or USP. This is what differentiates you from your competitors and your "About" page needs to make it clear.

I found an amazing blog post by Neil Patel that had a small infographic that wraps this up completely. Basically, it is 3 overlapping circles with a question in each.

1. What Your Brand Does Well

2. What The Consumer Wants

3. What Your Competitor Does Well

You want to only focus on delivering 2 of these items. You obviously don't want to say I know you want to buy a house & my competitor treats his clients amazingly. You also do not want to try and compare yourself to your competitor because this is YOUR about page! So the main two items you should focus on when thinking about your USP is... (What Your Brand Does Well) and (What The Customer Wants) ... If you are good at what you do then this should be basically the same thing.

Remember to think about your "About" page as an introduction to your potential customer. What part of your story and journey do you think is important to the connection between you and that awesome visitor that wants to be a customer?

Sketch Out Your About Page Design – You can work on the actual written content later...

Now that we have those two pages complete we are going to go over some of the other pages that you may want to use on your website. Because this book isn't for a specific industry I can't say you need "THIS" so I'm going to cover some of the most important pages in most industries aside from the home and about pages.

- Blog Page – This page doesn't require any design within Elementor. It will automatically display your recent blog posts (if you plan on blogging). The only thing you may want to consider is what you would like listed on the sidebar for your blog. But, we will be covering that in a little bit.

- Contact Page – Of course this page is important but aside from a few things you should have on this page it is basic. Yes you should have your contact information but you should make it easy for people to contact you with a form. If you have a physical location it would also help for you to have not only your address but use the map element to display a map of your location & possibly some directions from a major landmark if needed.

- Services Page – You may think it is enough to say that you are a painter but your services page will let your visitors know if you do drywall work/repair, deck staining and other things that you may believe to be understood as a painter. Listing the main services you offer helps people have peace of mind knowing you're not just saying "Yeah I can do that!" because you promote it and wouldn't promote something you haven't done before.

- Products Page – If you offer/sell products it always helps to have a page that does more than say that you sell cars. You should have a page that lists each of the products you have to offer with details for each product. If you only sell a small amount of products you may want to create a page for each product. Or if you own a store that has a lot of products, you may just want to have one products page that has a good overview of the type of products you have in your store.

- Portfolio Page – This could be used for many different industries including: graphic designers, painters, t shirt companies, artists, etc. This is basically a page to display your work. You can use individual images with small write ups about each "project" or you could even make it a page that displays a category "Portfolio" from your blog and do a new blog post for each of your portfolio items. Then they just see the featured image for that post and have to click to the blog post to read more information about that "project".

- FAQ Page (Frequently Asked Questions) – This may seem a little dated, but it works! Having a FAQ page will give you a bit of a resource section that you can send people to if they are asking a question about your process or maybe your turn around time. The most powerful part of the FAQ page is using it to acknowledge and address skepticism and objections to your products and/or services.

The next few pages are for you to brainstorm the pages you want to have as well as sketching out the design you would like to have on them. As you finish sketching your pages go over to your WordPress Dashboard. Click on Pages → Add New. Then start designing the pages.

Now that you know what you want your pages to look like, it's time to hop into your blog sidebar.

NOTE: If you do not plan on blogging you can skip this step. But, I don't recommend it. There are many benefits to blogging and I'd recommend that you take advantage of what is there.

When it comes to your side bar you will want to have a few things for sure:

- Search Box – If your going to be blogging you will want a way for people to search for the different posts within your blog. This is a must have for any active blogs.

- About Link or Short Bio – When you are blogging you will find that some people will find your posts before they look at your main pages on your website. So having a short bio and/or a link to your About page will let your blog readers know a little bit more about you than just being the person who wrote the blog.

- Popular Posts – After you've been blogging for a while you will find that there are 4-5 posts that are really popular and you should showcase these because if the majority of your readers like a select few posts more than others then why not drive more traffic to them.

- Recent Posts – This helps make the rabbit hole deeper. If your reader finds you via a blog post and they like what they read, they may want to read more and if you don't have an easy way to send them to more content you may lose out on getting them as a customer.

- Contact Information – This doesn't have to be complicated. A simple text with your phone number, address & maybe a button to your contact page can be an easy step towards getting your visitor to becoming a lead/customer.

- RSS Subscription – This is a way for people to get emails any time you publish a blog post. It isn't hard to set up and is very helpful.

- Call-to-Action – You want to have a solid call-to-action in your sidebar to get them to take a step closer towards becoming a customer. This could be a simple (Call for a FREE Estimate) or (Click here to download our White-paper on X)

- Social Links – If you are using social links in your header you may not want to use this section for all of your social media links. Instead, you may want to use this to spotlight the top 2 or 3 social media sites you are active on the most. This will make sure you don't overwhelm them with links but still gets them to connect with you.

Of course, there are a ton of different things that aren't listed here that you might want to have on your sidebar. Don't feel like you can't be different and have something I don't have listed here. Remember this is your website, so make it yours.

Use the template on the next page to sketch out your sidebar.

There are 3 columns on the next page for 3 mock ups.

Now that you have an idea of what you want to have on your side bar it is time to go put it together. You get to the area for your side bar within your Dashboard by going to Appearance → Widgets

There are 2 Sidebars in this page. The default is to have a "Right Sidebar" I'd recommend that you keep it that way. Although if you like the sidebar being on the left then by all means … go right ahead. :)

The Right Sidebar section should already have a few widgets in it. Use this to implement what you want in your design.

Now is time to fully go over the Elementor Plugin.

The Ultimate Elementor Guide

WWW.DIGITOOLBAG.COM/ELEMENTOR

When it comes to building a website with WordPress there are a lot of different ways to get the look you want. For years as a professional freelance website designer, I've used widget based WordPress themes, free page builders, premium page builders and just about anything else you can think of.

For the longest time, I used the Salient WordPress Theme that came with the Visual Composer plugin. After hours of research trying to find the easiest way to build a website with WordPress I came across an awesome FREE plugin called "Elementor".

I used the free plugin for months before buying Elementor Pro. Since then I refuse to even consider building a website without using Elementor, for myself or my clients.

Elementor is a visual page builder plugin for WordPress enabling the creation of web pages in a live, visual way.

If you follow along with this guide you will learn what you need to know about using Elementor.

Next thing we are going to do is going into the process.

When you are building your pages with elementor you will click "Edit With Elementor" from the basic editor page.

Once you are in the Elementor page editor you have two different options "+" which will add a new section & "Add Template" which is a file icon. We are going to cover the sections, once you understand the sections then you'll know how to edit the templates.

"ADD NEW SECTION"

When you click on "Add New Section" you will then need to decide what structure you want. Better way to look at it is, how many columns you want inside of this "section" or "row".

While you are deciding how many columns each section will have you need to think about the content you are using and if it will look good within the row width.

Once you select your structure, it will add a blank structure. With the section selected (hover over the section and click in the middle of the blue tab in the middle at the top of the section), you will see the "Edit Section" on the left side of the page.

There are three different sections at the top of the "Edit Section".

Layout

Inside of the "Layout" section you can change the basic features.

Stretch Section: With this enabled, it will give you the "full width" look. This will stretch the background to the edge of the page.

Content Width: Unless you are looking for a specific look I'd recommend that you keep this "Boxed" with the default settings. (You can also use full width and edit the padding/margins if you want the content to be full width. We'll cover that in a bit.)

Columns Gap: This will let you have a space between the different columns. For simplicity I'd recommend leaving this Default.

Height: This works for sections that you want basic elements in with the background being bigger than just the element.

Content Position: This allows you to have the content positioned within the section at the top, middle or bottom of the section.

The next section is the "Structure" and since we already have that set when we added the section we can move on.

Style

Background: This is where you can set the color of the background along with setting a background image. If you are wanting to edit the background all you need to do is to click on the paintbrush icon.

Once you've activated the background section you will see a section where you can change the background color.

Underneath that, you can upload the background image. If you decide to use images for the background you should be sure that the width is 1200-1500px. Once again I also urge you to optimize your images. (TinyPNG.com)

When you set the background image you have a few options to customize.

Position: There isn't many reasons to change this unless you want a specific section to show for a parallax effect or something like that. For most instances I'd recommend leaving this as Default.

Attachment: This is where you can get the parallax scrolling effect where the content of the section will scroll and the background will stay fixed/stationary or scroll.

Repeat: If you are wanting a "tiled" background, this is the option.

Size: You can test the different settings for this but I'd strongly advise the "cover" setting.

Background Overlay: this has the same basic options but with an Opacity scroll bar. This is to set how transparent the image or color overlay will be.

Border: Should you decide to use a border you can chose the different border types. If you decide to use a border then the next option, after you select your border type, is to set the Border Radius.

Border Radius: This type of setting box is something you will see more of moving forward so please pay attention to this. On the right side of the box you will have a link button. This will link all of the sections together. So if you set the "Top" section to 45 then it will automatically change the other three sections. If you un-check the link button then you can set each of the sections separately. When it comes to borders, most of the time 3-5px works.

Box Shadow: This will allow you to add a drop shadow to this section. Use this to add a depth to your page.

Shape Divider: This is going to be how you add the fun transitions on your page. This can add a geometric feel to your website pages. You can customize each setting with a shape divider on the top or bottom.

Typography: This is another section you will see many times moving forward but it may be a bit different for the different elements. But for this, you will be editing the parent settings for all of the typography within this section.

Advanced

Margin: This will add spacing on the outside of the section. You will use this to add spacing above or below the section

Padding: This section will allow you to add a spacing to the inside of the section displaying more of the background and less of the content.

Unless you know what you are doing I'd recommend you not touch the Z-Index/CSS ID/CSS Classes.

"Entrance Animation" is the last and final setting in this section. This will add an animation as the chosen section displays above the fold.

Responsive: This section is where you will change how this section will be displayed on the different devices.

Reverse Columns: When you design your pages you may have a page that has two columns and when it pulls up on mobile or on a tablet the wrong widget is on top. Using this will do just as it says, it will reverse the columns.

Visibility

Hide On Desktop: Use this when the section is for your mobile or tablet visitors.

Hide On Tablet: Use this when the section is for your mobile or desktop visitors.

Hide On Mobile: Use this when the section is for your tablet or desktop visitors.

Custom CSS

If you are using this tutorial and know how to write CSS then by all means, use this section. If you don't know what CSS is, then I highly recommend that you do not touch this section or any other custom CSS section you come across moving forward.

Column Settings

In order to edit the column settings you will need to select the column by hovering over the column and clicking on the grey "edit column" button in the upper right hand corner of the desired column.

Layout

For this you can change a few settings but we're going to keep this very basic.

Column Width(%): This is in case if you want the selected column to be a different percentage than what it is currently. Just keep in mind that the column width settings need to total at 100%

Content Position: Once again, just like the section settings you can chose to have the content inside of the selected column positioned at the top, in the middle, or towards the bottom of the column.

Widgets Space & HTML Tags are not needed for doing our sites. If you are more advanced and know how to use these, by all means go ahead.

Style

This section is very similar but your only options here is your background, background overlay(only displays when you have customized your background), border, and typography.

Advanced

Margin: This will add spacing on the outside of the column. You will use this to add spacing on the top, bottom, or the sides of the column.

Padding: This section will allow you to add a spacing to the inside of the column displaying more of the background and less of the content.

Use the section below for any notes you may need before we break down the individual elements within the page builder.

Elementor Widget Walk-Through

Since you know how the sections(rows) and columns work, now is the time to get comfortable with the different elements and what each of them does. I am going to be covering the Elementor Pro elements, along with the elements that are specific for the theme that we are using.

We are going to be walking through each of the elements within elementor and covering what they do. Some of this will seem very repetitive, so you might find that the further down the list I go I may not cover everything as I don't want to make this just a compilation of copy & paste. So, please take the time to make yourself familiar with each of the elements before you move forward.

Basic Elements

Columns: This element is to add additional columns under another column. For example: you may want a "Hero" section on your home page with a headline at the top and underneath it, have two separate columns to have your logo on one side and some text with a button on the other. This is where you would add additional columns inside of the single column section.

Inside of the "Edit Section" you will be able to change out the structure as well as the basic "Layout" settings. The "Style" tab will work the same here as before and the Advanced will as well.

Heading: This is for your page headings. Think of this as your page titles and headings that need to stand out on the page.

Title: In the "Edit Heading" section on the left of the page you can add your title in the text box.

Link: If you want your heading to link out to a landing page or something else you would put the desired link in this section.

Size: You can change the basic size of your heading here via Small, Medium, Large, or XL.

HTML Tag: When it comes to the HTML Tag, the best way to look at a page is that it should only have ONE H1 tag then from there I'd recommend you layout the rest of the page like a pyramid, with the most important headings being H2 & H3 and go down the list as you need.

NOTE: DO NOT FORCE YOUR "KEYWORDS" INTO YOUR CONTENT JUST FOR SEO. BUILD YOUR PAGES WITH YOUR CUSTOMERS/VISITORS IN MIND FIRST. THEN WORRY ABOUT THE REST.

Alignment: This is the same as the word processors on almost every computer. You can chose to align left, center or right. You can also chose to "justify" your text.

Style/Title

Text Color: This is an easy one. You can customize your color to an exact color code if you need to match up with your brand colors.

Typography: This is one of the sections that we're going to be skipping a lot moving forward so please pay close attention now.

The typography settings consists of a decent amount of features.

Family: This is where, if you want, you can change the font that the text will display in. Because there are a lot of different fonts, not all fonts are available. You can however, use any of the basic fonts along with any of the google fonts.

Size: Remember that you need to set this to make it big enough for people to read. Don't make the font size below 14, it makes it hard to read and makes people leave the page without consuming your content. You can make your font fairly large just make sure you test the responsiveness for the size. (We will cover how to do responsive design later on)

Weight: This is the thickness of the font. You can chose Default, Normal & Bold. You can also select the thickness based on a scale of 100-900 with the lower the number the thinner the letters and the higher the number the thicker the letters & numbers.

Transform: This feature has a few different settings. Default (depending on if you kept the default settings) will leave everything just as you type it. The next option is Uppercase which will make every letter uppercase. Lowercase will make all letters lowercase. Capitalize will make the first letter of each word uppercase. Normal will also leave everything just as you type it.

Style: This is where you can change the style to Normal, Italic or Oblique.

Decoration: This is where you can add an underline, over-line or a line through the text.

Line-Height: This will make the line higher, so it will add space to the top and bottom of the text, making the space in between the lines of text larger.

Letter Spacing: This adds space in between each letter that will stretch out the text to fit a larger section.

Text Shadow: Very Basic, it adds a shadow behind the text.

Blend Mode: This will change how the text is displayed. There are a lot of options for this, I'm not going to go into these here, feel free to look around and see what they do & if any of them will work for you.

Advanced: Same as before.

Image: This is how you add images to your page. When you add the image element, it will automatically add a placeholder image. Simply hover over the image in the sidebar to the left and click on "Delete" Then upload your new image.

Image size: As long as you upload images in the size they need to be displayed then you can set this to "Full" if not then just make the setting that displays the best for you.

Alignment: Select how you want the image aligned.

Caption: If you want to add a caption under the image you can do so here.

Link to: This is where you can chose to link to the media file or link the image to a specific URL.

Style

Width: you can choose to only display your image to a specific width

Max Width: This is where you can set a default that will keep the Max Width set to a specific %

Opacity: You can use this to display the image at a specific % transparency.

Border Type: You can select the type of border that you want along with the width which is the thickness of your border should you chose a border.

Border Radius: This will allow you to round out the corners of the image. If you upload a square image you can use the border radius to round out the corners and make it a display as a circle.

Box Shadow: this will add a box shadow to the image. Don't worry, if you set the border radius then it will show the shadow appropriate to the radius you set.

Advanced Settings are the same and from this point forward I will only be covering the Style & Advanced Settings when they are specific to the element.

Text Editor: This is for bodies of text. The editor will run just like the majority of word processors.

Video: This is an easy way to embed videos into your WordPress website. Once you add the element, chose the source (YouTube, Self-Hosted, etc.) then enter the URL to the video you want to embed/display on your page.

Start/End Time: If you only want a small portion of the video to show then you can set the start and end time that will ensure you can control exactly what is shown.

The other video options include: Auto play, Mute, Loop, Player Controls, Video Info, Modest Branding, Suggested Videos, and Privacy Mode.

If you feel like it you can also add an Image Overlay to the video.

Style

When you are selecting your video you may need to change the ratio in order to match the video you're embedding. You can also control the Play Icon that overlays on your video.

Button

Remember this element! In my opinion, the button is the most under utilized element in all of the page builders available for WordPress.

I normally don't do anything with the "Type" I'd rather customize everything.

Text: This is the text that displays on the button. "Click Here" for example.

Link: This is the URL that the button will link to.

Alignment: Align left, right, or center. If you chose "Justify" it will stretch the button to the width of the column it is in.

Size: You can chose basic settings here for the size of the button.

Icon: This allows you to add an icon in before or after the text on the button.

Icon Spacing: This only displays when you have an icon selected. This will adjust the spacing between the icon and the text on the button.

Style: The options here are pretty self explanatory so we're going to move forward.

Divider: This will add a line to separate sections on your website. You can chose if you want a solid line, double, dotted or dashed. Then the rest of the settings is to customize the look of the divider.

Spacer: This just adds blank space. If you want a large area to just display the background or want some extra space in between the different elements you can use this to add that space, if you don't want to edit the margin for the element.

Google Maps: This is an awesome element for local/"Brick and Mortar" businesses. By just putting in your address you can embed a map without any coding and it also will let you control the "zoom level" for the map along with "height" which will be the size it displays on your page.

Icon: This is simple, it displays the icon of your choice either plain or with a frame/background. You can use the Link section to enter a URL you want it to link to.

PRO Elements

Posts: This is for building a "spotlight" for bog posts within a page. For example: you may want to show a spotlight of three or four of your most recent blog posts on your home page. The settings for this is very detailed so hang in there I'll try not to go into anything you don't need.

Layout

Skin: There are two options here.

The first is Classic which displays the Featured Image at the top, blog post title, date/comments, summary with a "read more" link. This looks more like the traditional layout you might have seen hundreds of times over the last few years.

The second option "Cards" is a clean and modern look. It showcases the featured image with a badge that shows the category. You can also display the Gravatar (Image of the author, setup via gravatar.com). This also displays looking like "cards" with all the info just sitting on the page with the default settings it adds a drop shadow.

Columns: This is where you select how many columns you want to display your blog posts. You can display more than just the amount of columns by utilizing the Posts per page setting below just a quick heads up. Keep it clean and don't go over three or four columns.

Posts Per Page: Like I said above you can have separate rows of posts. Depending on what you are using the section for you can set up with three columns and set the (PPP) to six which will display two rows of three.

Show Image: This will allow you to display the featured image for each post or not.

Masonry: Using the Masonry setting will allow you to display the entire featured image and will have the cards/posts display like the Masonry layout. Kind of like bricks are laid sort of uneven.

Image Size: You can customize your image size here if you feel the need to. Once again, be sure to optimize your images for mobile. (TinyPNG.com)

Image Ratio: If you are not seeing the full image you can use the image ratio to display the full image depending on the ratio of your image.

For the rest of the settings you can turn on or off each of the features within the element. I don't want to fill you up with fluff so please click around and make yourself familiar with the settings.

Portfolio: This will work the same as the Posts element. Only difference is that it only shows the image.

Slides: Just as it sounds, this a "Slider" element.

Form: This is my top reason for my recommendation to buy the Elementor Pro plugin. With this element, it allows you to create extremely professional looking forms with integration to software like MailChimp and GetResponse. You can also use this just as a basic contact form that just sends the submissions to your email. There are a lot of different settings and ways to customize your forms. I recommend that you take a look at the Elementor channel on YouTube. There is a great collection of videos including an amazing walk-through on how to customize your forms with Elementor.

Note: From this point moving forward, you should have a good understanding of the editor section. I will be covering the basic features of each element and if you need any more information on the elements, feel free to check out the Elementor Docs overview page located at: https://docs.elementor.com.

Login: For most websites you wouldn't want a login form because you can use the default login page. But if you are building something like a membership site, you can create a login form for your members/users.

Nav Menu: This will be used to display a horizontal menu for your header & footer. (We kind of already covered this.)

Animated Headline: This is used just like the Headline in the basic elements we discussed earlier but this adds fun animation effects to a specific part of the headline. For example: It can add an animated text effect like a keyboard typing, flipping and other animation intros. You can also select to add an animated circle, underline, strike through and others to a specific part of the text by entering the animated part of the headline into "Highlighted Text". To change the color of the animated circle, underline, etc., you can do so under the "Style" tab.

Price List: this has a restaurant menu style to list products, brief descriptions along with prices. Items can be added, duplicated or removed via List edit section in the left sidebar.

Price Table: This is the fancy graphic that you see on sales pages that list the product along with the price and the benefits with a call-to-action button.

Flip Box: This is the box you see that has a flip style animation when you hover over it, revealing different content on the back of the box.

Call To Action: This is a clean box that has an image(for the product/service) with a headline, small summary, and then a button to send traffic to a specific URL.

Media Carousel: This helps you make a fancy slideshow of images, a scrolling image carousel and a few other options. You can also use this to display video's. The best option is to upload videos you want to use on YouTube then use the YouTube link in the video link options.

Testimonial Carousel: Just as it sounds. The only thing I would recommend is keep the testimonials limited to no more than four. You don't want the animations to slow down the loading speed of your site and not to mention, almost no one will spend the time to scroll through that many testimonials. I'd also suggest you link to your reviews tab on your Facebook page.

Countdown: This is a fun element. You can use this inside of blog posts to show an expiration of a deal or special you are running. You can also have a countdown to an event you are hosting, along with a lot of other uses.

Share Buttons: These give you share buttons for the different platforms like Facebook, Twitter, Pinterest, LinkedIn, and others.

Block Quote: This showcases a quote that includes an optional Tweet Button to share the quote from your website.

Facebook Button: This adds a "Like" button to your page for people to like the page they are on.

Facebook Comments: This will add a comment section on your page that is fully integrated with Facebook.

Facebook Embed: This is how you embed an individual post from your Facebook page. You can also embed a specific Facebook comment or video.

Facebook Page: This is the "traditional" Facebook Like Box. It displays your page in a condensed layout.

Template: This is where you can embed the templates you design within the Elementor settings. (You access this via Dashboard>Elementor>My Templates)

General Elements

Image Box: This is a simple content box with an image, title, and description.

Icon Box: This is the same as the image box but with an icon instead of an image.

Image Gallery: This is a basic image gallery.

Image Carousel: This is similar to the media carousel but with a cleaner look (in my opinion)

Icon List: This is great for listing benefits or contact information. You can have a bullet list that will just have icons for the bullets so you can chose the icon you want displayed instead of just the boring bullet. (•)

Counter: An animated number with a title. Good for listing how many projects you've worked on.

Progress Bar: Simply displays a title with a progress bar with name and %.

Testimonial: This is a basic testimonial element that showcases a testimonial.

Tabs: Using this element will allow you to have multiple tabs displaying different content within your page. There is no limit to tabs you can have but I'd recommend keeping to where there is only one row of titles in the tabs.

Accordion: Similar to the Tabs element, the Accordion will be a drop down with content between the titles. This opens up each section one at a time.

Toggle: A similar look and feel as the Accordion but allows the visitor to toggle all "tabs"

Social Icons: This is a clean element that will let you display the different social media icons to represent your different profiles and accounts.

Alert: This will give a semi-temporary alert to visitors that they can close out. This works for good call-to-action's and news for your business.

SoundCoud: For musicians this allows you to embed a song from your SoundCoud account.

Shortcode: This is for putting shortcodes on your page. Shortcodes are used by WordPress, Themes & Plugins to reference different content & normally look like [this].

HTML: This is where you are able to put in raw HTML code.

Menu Anchor: This is to link to different parts on your page. Please reference the Elementor Docs for more information.

Sidebar: This allows you to put in a sidebar into your page to display widgets.

Site Elements & WordPress Elements

These elements are self explanatory so we will not be going into these elements.

Use these elements for basic edits in adding content throughout your page. You will find a lot of different things you can use in customizing your page.

Now that you have a decent understanding of the different elements and now we are going to go over the four icons that are at the bottom of the edit sidebar.

The first is General settings which allows you to edit the page title, publication status, featured image, You can hide the title and also select your page layout.

The second icon is the responsive icon: More on this in a little bit

The third icon is to go back in "history" and undo edits. So be careful with this one.

The fourth icon is to view a preview of the page.

Last but not least is the Publish Button. If you click on the arrow to the right you will be able to save it as a draft or as a template.

Responsive Website Design

Now we are going to go over our pages in Tablet and Mobile mode to test the responsiveness of your website.

Responsive Web Design is about using HTML and CSS to automatically resize, hide, or enlarge, a website, to make it look good on all devices (desktops, tablets, and phones).

Lucky for you, Elementor allows you to do this without having to write or edit any code.

In order to view and edit the website to make it responsive you will need to go to the bottom of the edit sidebar and click on the responsive icon. It is an icon of a computer monitor.

This will open up the options for you to view your website in Desktop, Tablet, or Mobile.

Since we are doing the full build in Desktop by default, the next thing we are going to do is to select the Tablet preview.

Now you need to look over the content and make the changes need to font sizes, padding and margins in order to make it look the way you want it to. After you make the changes needed you need to do the same thing with the Mobile preview.

Follow the steps needed to complete the design of your website.

Congratulations! You have built your own website!

But We're Far From Done!

Now that we have your website built, we need to cover a few very important things.

☐   Double Check your Content

Take a few minutes and make sure your content is good to go. Double check your spelling, grammar and all that fun stuff. (you can use a free browser extension called Grammarly) I'd also recommend that you share your website with some close friends or family members to get some extra eyes on your content just to be safe.

☐   Update WordPress, Theme & Plugins

The latest releases for WordPress itself along with your theme and plugins are normally released for security reasons. Be sure to keep everything up to date. The majority of the updates are basic and are at no risk to crashing your site. Unfortunately, sometimes you may find that an update can crash your site so be sure to backup your site using the Duplicator plugin. (For more information & a tutorial for using duplicator to backup your website visit www.digitoolbag.com/duplicator)

☐   Responsive Website Check

Take a few minutes and go through all of the pages you've designed with the desktop, tablet & mobile layouts. This is very important. You want to make sure all of your pages are responsive and look right on all platforms. (I'd also look into Kproxy.com which will show you an uncached version of your site and what it looks like on different platforms.)

☐   Cross Browser Compatibility

You can use any tool you want to do this. If you do a search on Google for "cross browser compatibility check" you will find a huge list including the free tool I use: browserling.com. If you want to get a little more "hands on" you can manually open up each of the different browsers and check yourself, but I'd recommend using a tool and saving yourself some time.

☐ Secure Your Website

Go to WhyNoPadlock.com and make sure that you are 100% secure. If you followed along then you should be good to go but unfortunately sometimes there are a few issues that come up. But, good news for you, using WhyNoPadlock.com will tell you exactly what you need in order to get that green padlock we all want to see.

☐ Change The Admin Email

In your general settings inside of your dashboard, you will find your "Admin Email". Make sure that you add an email that you check on a regular basis. This is going to be where they email you all of your notifications for your website.

☐ Page Speed Test

You should be fine with this if you followed along and optimized all of your images with TinyPNG.com. To run the test, you need to go to GTMetrix.com. Put in your URL with the proper protocol (https://). This may be a little complicated for you to understand at first just know you need to aim for an A "grade" for your Page Speed and Yslow score but if you can't get it … a B is not going to be the end of you. You can use "Cloudflare" to speed your site up if you feel the need for it. Setting up a CDN (Content Delivery Network) like Cloudflare can be difficult and like I've said many times before, I want to keep this book to the basics so I'm not going to cover Cloudflare here but you can get the tutorial at digitoolbag.com/cloudflare

☐ Check all links (internal & external)

Nothing is worse than sending traffic to your website only for them to find something they want to get more information on and when they click the link, nothing happens. So take a few minutes and click on every link on your site and make sure they go where you want them to.

☐ SEO Site Check

This isn't an easy check. SEO is a beast and at times you may feel like there is no way that you could keep up with all of the algorithms but if you continue to put out content that is for the readers & visitors of your website first, you will be fine. In the back of this workbook is an SEO Crash Course. I hope it helps.

☐ Disable Coming Soon Page

If you chose to set up a coming soon page, now is when you go over to the settings and disable it. Now, The World Can See Your Website!!! Yay!!

☐   Backup Website

There are a lot of ways to backup your WordPress Website. I recommend a free plugin that I've used for a while called "Duplicator". It isn't difficult to use and can not only backup your website but can be used to clone websites to move to new servers etc. I use this for WebDesignWebinar.com to create a shortcut. If you need more information on it you can check out the post: DigiToolBag.com/duplicator

☐   Launch Your Website

Now that you have finished building your website, all you need to do is tell people!

Don't forget to share your website on your social media profiles and be sure to tweet @ me with the link so I can see your website. @cjhallock

Moving forward, be sure to check back with www.FreeWebDesignTutorial.com for more tutorials & updates. You can also get all resources that you need along with templates for marketing your business/website via social media and more at DigiToolBag.com

Disclaimer: Links inside of this guide may or may not result in compensation if you take action based on my recommendation

Bonus SEO Chapter

The first goal of any search engine optimization strategy is to get your website and all pages indexed. But even before that can happen, you need to get the search engine crawlers to visit your website. Depending on the search engine or directory and the overall circumstances (how you invite and solicit crawlers), that first visit could take days, weeks, or even months.

While it's true that the initial crawler visits can be somewhat unpredictable (or take a long time in coming), once the ice is broken, future visits can be controlled to some degree…

Basically, the more frequently you update your pages, the more frequently the crawlers will show up on your website doorstep. Which is one of the reasons I recommend blogging on a regular basis, but more on that later.

Of course, that's only half the battle. The other half is getting the search engines and directories to actually index your pages.

In order to do that, you need to start at the beginning. And the beginning in this particular instance is developing and enhancing pages in such a way that the search engine crawlers will be impressed.

The overall search process is simple…

All the text content that search engine crawlers gather is stored and indexed. People conduct searches based on certain phrases (keywords). Whatever content possesses the most relevancy with regard to any given keyword will be placed in the top positions of the search results.

Since the title of the page and the text content generally carry the most weight - at least with regard to what search engine crawlers deem most relevant during their visits - it stands to reason that improvement in page rank and/or search results listing can most often be attributed to having individual and specific keywords properly incorporated into those two prime areas.

Of course, if keywords were the only basis for which page rank and position in search results were determined, optimizing web pages would be pretty much cut and dried…

Pick a keyword > use it in your title and throughout your content >

achieve high page rank and top position in search engine results

The problem is, there are so many variables that not only come into play but change on a regular basis, it can seem as though achieving solid and effective search engine optimization might never be possible.

Fortunately, it's not only possible, it can be relatively painless as well. All you have to do is satisfy the top three requirements of pretty much all major search engines…

- Provide quality content

- Update content on a regular basis

- Get numerous top-ranking websites to link back to your site

The search engines and directories you should be trying to impress the most are the top three contenders…

1. Google

2. Bing

3. Yahoo

Beyond that, there are countless other search engines and directories.

Should you optimize for those as well, or simply level your sites on the major players and bypass all the search engines and directories below them? Not necessarily. You still want your pages listed in as many locations as possible. You just shouldn't try to satisfy every one of them with regard to optimization.

Satisfy the top contenders. Then, if you have the time and ambition to broaden the scope of your SEO efforts, do it. If not, don't worry about the hundreds (or even thousands) of other search engines and directories that exist.

You're only human. And just meeting the optimization criteria of the top three is going to be challenging and energetic enough.

Of course, unless you plan to make search engine optimization your life's work, it's not likely you'll invest most of your energy in that one single area (even when restricted to the top three players). But you do need to invest a fair amount of quality effort.

That basically equates to these two missions…

1. Get your pages indexed by major search engines.

2. Improve your page rank and position in search results.

In order to accomplish both of those, you need to carefully balance the line between good optimization techniques and the urge to take things a bit too far.

In other words, you need to make certain you carry out your two missions without stepping over the line into what's commonly referred to as "black hat" search engine tactics.

That dark and evil territory would include things like…

Keyword Stuffing - repeating keywords over and over again for no logical or practical reason

Hidden Content - including keywords or text that's the same color as the background for the purpose of manipulating search engine crawlers

Doorway Pages - not intended for viewers to see but rather to trick search engines into placing the website into a higher index position

Although these types of practices were once considered intelligent and effective methods of optimization, they can now result in having your website banned from search engines entirely and unfortunately forever.

In general, it's better to concentrate on the most popular and most reasonable optimization techniques. By doing that, you'll not only achieve the results you're looking for, your efforts will have long lasting results.

When you consider how much work is involved in getting any website to the top of search engine rank and position, it's worth whatever effort it takes to get it right the first time.

Search Engine Strategy Basics

For the most part, there are three basic things you'll need to do in order to accomplish proper and effective search engine optimization.

- Compile keyword lists

- Publish keyword-rich content

- Establish a beneficial link strategy

Keywords

The core of any SEO strategy is built almost entirely around the group of keywords you choose to target.

The first order of business is to decide which groups of keywords you'll be utilizing. In most instances, those groups will be either directly or indirectly related to the topic or niche that your website is (or will be) associated with.

Once you've established the individual groups of keywords you want to target, you can begin to compile a comprehensive list of top-level phrases that have each of the following characteristics:

- Are searched for by thousands of viewers each and every month

- Have little or no competition associated with it

The more people who search for the term combined with the least amount of competition associated with it, the more valuable the keyword will be with regard to gaining automatic search engine traffic.

Beyond that, you'll want to compile lists of secondary keywords. These would still be valuable, but not to the extent that the first top-level list would be.

The main advantage of lower level keywords is the fact that you don't have to work quite as hard to get definitive search engine recognition. And since you'll automatically get fairly decent results position, you'll also receive additional targeted viewer traffic.

To make up for the lack of quality in the keyword itself (in most cases that equates to fewer searches being conducted every month and therefore less competition), you need to work with a much larger quantity of lower-level keywords.

Basically, the results will be just as good as what you experience through top-level keywords. It will just take more keywords to achieve those same results.

There are several ways in which you can compile keyword lists. One of the quickest and easiest methods is to use is Google & their keyword planner.

Now, I would love to go over all the steps to use the keyword planner but I really don't want to take up more time than I need to so I'd recommend you taking a look at this overview:

www.digitoolbag.com/keyword-planner

Quality Content

There are numerous reasons why "Content Is King".

From a viewer's perspective, content not only invites them to visit your website but encourages them to return on a regular basis.

It's a relatively simple equation…

They're looking for valuable information. Give it to them.

From a search engine perspective, content is one of the primary factors in determining just how much weight or importance should be given to any web page.

Unfortunately, this one isn't quite as simple an equation…

Search engine crawlers gather and index content. Figure out how to make them place your content higher on the results ladder than some other website.

Of course, in order to become King, content needs to be of considerable quality. In order to remain King, content needs to be updated on a fairly regular basis.

Not to mention the fact that you also need to add content (new pages) on a regular basis. If not, whatever ground you initially gain will simply fade away. And so will whatever search position or rank you've achieved.

Linking Strategies

Choosing the right keywords and publishing quality keyword-rich content puts you approximately two-thirds of the way toward optimum search engine recognition. The other third is pretty much solely based on popularity.

If we were talking about popularity in the real world, it would probably include simple things like who was voted King and Queen of the high school prom, or who had the most date options on a Saturday night, or which sibling got the most attention from Mom or Dad.

In the world of search engines, popularity takes on a whole different meaning. And in most instances, it comes down to this… the website with the most quality links pointing to it wins the contest.

Link popularity

That's the game. And the ultimate goal is to get countless "important" websites (those that have a theme or topic that's similar to yours) to provide links back to you. Of course, when we're talking about importance, we're referring to how major search engines view them.

Most often, that equates to high page rank and top position in search results. The higher up the food chain a website happens to be, the more powerful any link they provide back to you is perceived.

In order to get the most bang out of the link popularity process, it's best if you actually seek out valuable websites. Aside from those you might already have in mind, conduct searches based on the keywords you're most interested in gaining search engine recognition for.

Naturally, someone who's in direct competition with you wouldn't even consider giving you a link back. So what you've really looking for are popular websites that have content or products that are either complimentary to yours or are indirectly.

For example, let's say your topic and keyword is based on ways of perfecting your golf swing. Good link back choices would be websites with the following themes or products:

- Information about golf courses or golf tournaments

- Golf equipment or apparel

- Golf instructors or seminars

If the topic is related to yours and the website that's providing the link back carries a good deal of weight with major search engines, the value of your own website will automatically be elevated.

When it comes to the actual link that these valuable and important websites place on their pages…

Always encourage the use of text links rather than just a URL. For example, instead of simply displaying http://www.digitoolbag.com as the link back to your website, you want something more substantial and keyword rich. And, of course, search engine friendly.

If one of your keywords is "targeted traffic", for example, the link might read as follows:

Get Exclusive Marketing & Webdesign Tools & Resources With DigiToolBag Free Membership.

That not only gives you credit for the keyword, it encourages the search engine crawler to perceive your website as having more value.

Always keep in mind that in this particular instance, quality will always win out over quantity. Yes, you want a vast number of links pointing back to your website. But given a choice, you're much better off with fewer links from important websites than countless links from sites that don't carry much weight with search engines.

NOTE: While backlinks are important in getting ranked for your desired keywords, only real links are good for you. So please head my advice when I say DO NOT UNDER ANY CIRCUMSTANCES BUY BACKLINKS. While I fully support sites like Fiverr, there are always bad apples. When you buy backlinks, especially in bulk, there is no guarantee.

Basic Overview...

Most search engines use meta description and keyword tags. High score for the overall weight and proximity of keywords, < h > tags, and bold text. Rewards quality content, anywhere between 500 to 1600 words. Content should include keywords in text and links. Likes to see keywords in the page title (utilizing 90 characters or less) and carried consistently throughout the website. Especially values link popularity, themes, and keywords in URL's and link text. The use of excessive keywords, cloaking, and link farms is viewed as spamming and/or "BlackHat SEO".

<u>*What Not To Do...*</u>

After all your hard work getting your web pages optimized, the last thing you want is to do something that would prevent your site from getting indexed. Or worse, have it blacklisted by search engines altogether.

At the top of the "don't do" list is the use of invisible text (the text is the same color as the background). Most every search engine is wise to this practice and will currently ban any website found to be using it.

Here is a quick rundown of everything else you should never do...

- Don't repeat keywords excessively.

- Don't place irrelevant keywords in the title and meta tags.

- Don't make use of link farms.

- Don't submit to inappropriate categories in search directories.

- Don't submit too many web pages in one day.

- Don't publish identical pages.

- Don't use meta refresh tags

No matter how good your website is - no matter how valuable the content it contains or how legally optimized it might be - if you use any of the things spelled out above, you run the risk of being blacklisted, branded as a search engine spammer.

Although it varies from one search engine to another, spamming can include one or more of the following:

- Irrelevant web page titles and meta description and keywords tags

- Repetition of keywords

- Hidden or extremely small text

- Submitting web pages more than once in a twenty-four-hour span

- Mirror sites that point to different URL addresses

- Using meta refresh tags

When it comes to directories such as DMOZ (which have human editors), spamming generally equates to one of these three practices: deliberate choice of an inappropriate category within the directory; marketing language; capitalization of letters

It's not difficult to stay out of black hat territory. But it's certainly difficult to recover from having used those types of techniques. That is, assuming you can recover at all.

Just pay attention to the rules established by search engines and directories. And since Google is the player you'll most want to satisfy, it's important that you read and re-read their webmaster guidelines which are published at http://www.google.com/webmasters/ on a regular basis.

Break the rules and you'll always be struggling to gain benefit from all the major search engines. Follow the rules and you'll establish web pages that will not only be around a long time, they'll always be in contention for top search results position.

Now that we have gone through that … WE ARE DONE!

Thank you for spending this time with me! If I can help you moving forward be sure to shoot me a tweet or DM on Instagram:

@cjhallock

Be Great & Stay Boosted,

We'll see you at the top!

CJ Hallock